New Game Cuisine

Selected Menus and Suggested Wines

By Janet Hazen

Wine Notes by Brian St. Pierre

Photography by Joyce Oudkerk Pool

Design by Thomas Ingalls

Chronicle Books • San Francisco

Printed in Japan.

Library of Congress Cataloging-in-Publication
Data

    Hazen, Janet.
       New game cuisine / Janet Hazen ; photo-
    graphs by Joyce Oudkerk Pool ; wine notes by
    Brian St. Pierre.
         p.   cm.
       Includes bibliographical references (p.   )
    and index.
       ISBN 0-87701-717-4. — ISBN 0-87701-
    677-1 (pbk.)
       1. Cookery (Game)   2. Cookery (Wine)
    I. Title   II. Title: New game cuisine
      TX751.H4 1990
      641.6′91—dc20   90-2187
                                 CIP

Distributed in Canada by Raincoast Books, 112
East Third Avenue, Vancouver, B.C. V5T 1C8

Book Design: Ingalls + Associates
Food Stylist: Barbara Berry
Assistant Food Stylist: Gina Francis Farruggio
Editing: Carolyn Miller
Composition: Wilsted & Taylor

10 9 8 7 6 5 4 3 2 1

Chronicle Books
275 Fifth Street
San Francisco, California 94103

I would like to thank the Game Exchange for their superior products, extra-special service, and support.

Special thanks to all my friends and family for tasting these menus.

Thanks to Jim Heubner for sharing his beautiful pheasant and enthusiastic knowledge of game hunting.

To Mary Ingalls for the unending supply of Minnesota wild rice and for lending us her beautiful cookware.

To Dr. Ed Ingalls for teaching his son to hunt and how to prepare various kinds of wild birds.

A special thank you to the wine merchants who helped select particular bottles and vineyards to match our wine suggestions. They include The Wine House, Connoisseur Wine, Mager Cheese & Wine, and Kermit Lynch Wine Merchants.

A very special thank you to Dennis Lapuyade and Stephen Singer of Singer & Foy Wines for their support and advice throughout the development of this book.

and
The Gardener
Chris Krisov
Kathryn Holm
John Lyons
Mary Lyons
Jane Fehon—Props
Daniel Bowe—Props
Debra Casserly—Assistant
Joe Ashton—Assistant
Emily Harvey
To Fred, who made it through this cookbook

CONTENTS

INTRODUCTION

Imagine your kitchen, warm and cozy, the air heavy with the unmistakable aroma of duck roasting in the oven. Or picture a breezy summer afternoon in the backyard, the outdoor grill filled with tiny quail or juicy buffalo steaks. A plump, perfectly roasted game bird makes as good an invitation for feasting as anything I can think of. A braised rabbit dish or perhaps lean, butter-tender venison tenderloin is equally tempting. Choosing which to serve is the biggest problem, for once you acquire a taste for the addictive qualities of game, you will be forever thinking of new and different ways to prepare these delicacies.

Game was one of our first foods, keeping tribes of hunter-gatherers alive during the long winters of the paleolithic age. Because it was both essential and elusive, dangerous and sustaining, game and the relationship of humans to it was a major source of mythology and culture.

Today we are far removed from the world of wild animals, and until recently game has been, for most of us, an exotic rarity, available only to hunters. Due to the advent of game farms, this is rapidly changing. Quail, partridge, squab, pheasant and grouse, buffalo, deer, and other game animals and wild fowl are being raised for the market, and are available to the public through a growing network of specialty food companies, specialty meat markets, and mail order food companies.

Game is part of the quiet revolution in farming over the last few years that has given us not only organically raised specialty vegetables, but such formerly "wild" foods as oysters, catfish, and wild mushrooms. Farms such as Broken Arrow Ranch in Texas grow free-range game that is sold to restaurants and retail companies. Unlike most of our commercially raised meat and poultry, free-range game is free of hormones, steroids, and antibiotics. Free-range meat and fowl are also lower in fat and thus lower in calories. And because these animals and birds are raised under natural conditions, not only is their flesh healthier for humans to eat, it is richer in flavor.

Animals and birds in the wild eat and live naturally, which makes their meat taste better. The antibiotics, chemicals, and vitamins injected into most commercially raised animals also make their meat less desirable from a health standpoint. If you are a meat eater, you may want to consider the way in which animals are raised. This book is not centered around moral, social, political, or health issues, but it must be acknowledged that hunting animals is a controversial subject with many people. Then consider, if you will, the lifestyle of an animal or bird living naturally in the open, shot quickly by the hunter, then used for food. Or, alternatively, game that is raised on farms in large outdoor pens, fed naturally, and slaughtered for the wholesale market. The more common alternative is the bird or animal that is raised in a tiny, dark pen and fed chemicals. Suffice it to say, dining on wild or free-range fowl or game from time to time is a sound and healthy way to eat.

Some Americans grew up hunting, cleaning, and cooking wild fowl and game. But for most of us, this category of food is unfamiliar. This is not a book to teach you about hunting, dressing, or cleaning game, but a book of recipes that will tell you what you need to know about an entirely new area of cooking.

Europe, China, India, and the Middle East consider wild fowl and game standard fare; Latin America has also embraced this food that is rich in tradition and history. Game is not only unfamiliar to most Americans, but it has the reputation in this country of having a "gamey," or overly strong flavor. It is true that game, unlike much traditional American food, is not bland. Most wild fowl and game have assertive, distinct flavors that are preferred by those who truly enjoy the passions of the table.

This "new" category of food is thus being seen more and more often on the tables of some of our most innovative chefs, who have incorporated game into the list of foods important to the new American cuisine. And now game is available to the home cook as well, through retail suppliers. High-quality butcher shops and specialty meat markets are beginning to carry game. As these foods become more popular, we will see wild fowl and game with more frequency and in greater quantities. When the public demands new ingredients, it is the responsibility of retailers to provide their customers with what they want, whenever possible. If you do not have a good source for wild game or fowl or even good produce, try talking to the buyer or manager of your local butcher, grocery, or produce store. Chances are he or she will do what can be done to please you and retain you as a satisfied customer.

Another source for farm-raised game and free-range domesticated animals and fowl may be close to your own backyard. A growing number of small farms are beginning to raise a variety of stock by natural means. Often you can locate locally raised game by connecting with a farm trails system, in which a group of farmers band together to publicize their products.

But even cooks who don't have access to game in the market or from the farmer can order fresh game by telephone from companies that carry a range of foods including quail, squab, venison, wild boar, and buffalo. Some sources also offer smoked game, duck fat, and other specialty foods. Any of these products can be delivered to your door within twenty-four hours, packed in insulated boxes. For a list of these mail- and phone-order companies, see "Sources for Game and Specialty Foods" in the back of this book.

Because game meats and wild fowl are unfamiliar to many cooks, some may think that these foods are difficult to prepare or that they are acquired tastes. Game has an undeserved reputation for being overly assertive in flavor, but the truth is that the clear and distinct tastes of game can bring back to our cuisine the character it has lost over the years of over-breeding and pen-raising animals and poultry. And, as you will find, game is no more difficult to cook than any other kind of meat.

This book provides you with a glossary of game and other specialty meats. The definitions of the words "game" and "wild fowl" have become blurred in this era of farm-raising birds and animals formerly wild. We have expanded our menus to include some foods that technically are not truly game, such as free-range chicken, capon, poussin, and Cornish game hens, because these birds are raised naturally under the same conditions as farm-raised game and are available through the same sources. In many cases they can be substituted for game in specific recipes, and vice versa. The majority of the menus in this book are based on fowl, but recipes for rabbit, wild boar, buffalo, and venison are included. The front matter of the book has a section on basic cooking techniques, with attention focused on game. A section of stocks, sauces, marinades and stuffings follows. Recipes for appetizers, soups, and salads, many of which use cooked game, are next.

Each menu is designed around one kind of game or specialty meat, with the accompanying dishes chosen to complement the main dish. The menus draw inspiration from a wide range of cuisines such as Italian, French, Greek, Latin American, Asian, American, and Middle Eastern. The recipes reflect the long European tradition of game cookery, transformed by the new American emphasis on a variety of ethnic flavors and innovative combinations of ingredients. The produce in each menu is fairly consistent with the season, so you won't be asked to find raspberries to go along with turnips and winter squash in the same meal. Most menus serve four to six people with generous portions, sometimes with leftovers, but it is always safe to use portion suggestions as a guideline, not as a rule. Some menus feature a soup or an appetizer; these may be omitted for a lighter meal, but quite often a small bowl of soup or a light appetizer adds elegance to what would otherwise be a simple meal.

I have found through teaching cooking that the most common problem for the home cook is planning a menu that works. It is one thing to come up with an interesting appetizer or vegetable dish, but to organize an entire meal is more difficult. Colors, textures, size of portions, food compatibility, and, most of all, flavor must be considered when planning a menu. All the elements play against and with each other to make a satisfying meal of stimulating and memorable dishes. Each component has an equally important role in the success of the individual dish and the meal as a whole. I think you will find these menus diverse, straightforward, and unique.

A wine suggestion for each menu is listed below the recipe titles. Because game is one of our original foods and wine is one of our oldest beverages, we believe that the pairing of wine and game is a heritage worth honoring. Brian St. Pierre, who writes about food and wine among many other topics, has contributed an essay on how to choose wine for a specific dish of game, including his own recommendations. Most menus give a choice of two wines, often one European and one American. If you cannot find the wines suggested simply ask your wine merchant to recommend one that is similar. Certainly if you have your favorite wine picked out to go with a particular meal and you feel that it will complement the food, go with it. There are no hard and fast rules when it comes to enjoying food and wine.

Wild fowl and game are common food for some, exotic and rare for others. If you have been cooking with wild fowl and game for a while you can use this book for inspiration and new ideas, or you can choose recipes for dishes that use your favorite ingredients. If this is a new world of cooking to you, I hope you will proceed with a curious mind and palate, an empty belly, and a home full of hungry family members and friends. I guarantee you will find a rewarding new cuisine.

When I was growing up, from time to time my mother would say despairingly, after a trip to the grocery store, "I wish they would invent another kind of meat to cook." With the world of game open to us again, it's as if my mother's wish has finally been granted. I hope this book will help you to make the most of the possibilities of this cuisine. I wish you enjoyment and many good feasts.

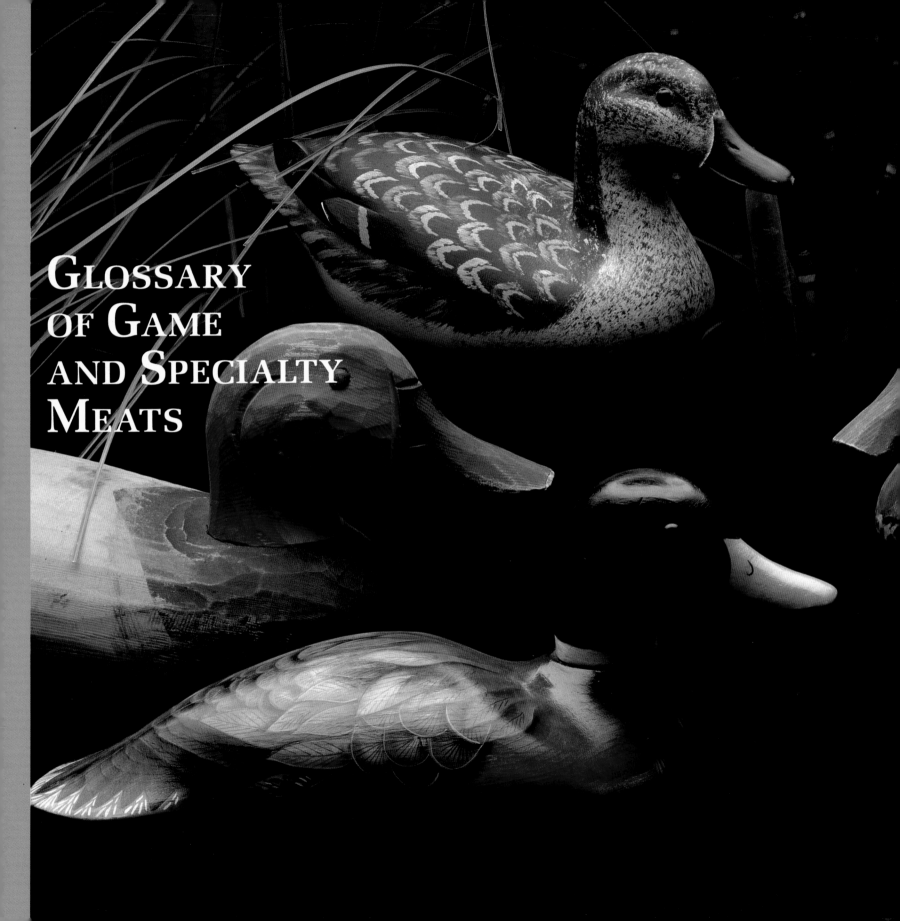

GLOSSARY OF GAME AND SPECIALTY MEATS

Glossary of Game and Specialty Meats

Buffalo

Buffalo, correctly called American bison, can be treated in much the same way as beef. Although the taste of buffalo meat is similar to beef, it is leaner and more full-flavored, and the same cut of meat can be quite different. Buffalo New York steaks, for example, are flatter, smaller, and much less fatty than their beef counterpart. In most circumstances, buffalo can be cooked in the same manner as beef.

Capon

Capon has been domesticated for centuries, but it can be used in place of an adult pheasant in most recipes. A castrated male chicken, the average capon weighs approximately 6 to 8 pounds. The flesh is slightly stringy and is flavorful and rich. Capon has both white and dark meat and may be cooked in any of the ways chicken is cooked. It is especially good roasted and makes a rich stock for soup. The skin of a fresh young capon will be tight and resilient and the breastbone flexible.

Cornish Game Hen

Cornish game hens are domesticated fowl, the result of crossbreeding the Cornish gamecock and the Plymouth Rock hen. These all-white-meat birds weigh 1 to 2 pounds. A diet consisting of acorns and cranberries imparts a unique and delicious overtone to the flesh. A Cornish game hen is more flavorful than a chicken, but much more delicate than wild fowl. These birds are available frozen in many supermarkets and most poultry shops, and are found fresh in some specialty markets. Birds ranging in age from 5 to 7 weeks are preferred because the meat is more tender than on older birds. The breastbone of a young hen will be soft and pliable, and the skin will be springy. Cornish game hens may be used in place of poussins, although they are generally a bit larger. They may also be substituted for baby pheasant and squab. Traditionally roasted, they are also good marinated and grilled over wood or charcoal.

Duck

There are many varieties of wild and domestic duck, and each has a distinctive character. Their one common characteristic is their rich and rewarding flavor. All domestic and some wild ducks have a high percent of fat and large frames. This should be kept in mind when planning a meal, as one small duck is almost big enough for two people, but too much for one.

Domestic ducks are available either frozen or fresh in many grocery stores and poultry shops. Most Pekin or Long Island ducks are 7 to 8 weeks old and weigh about 4 to 5 pounds. Both develop a thick layer of fat, which makes for a tender and juicy bird but one with little meat. Muscovy is one of the largest ducks, weighing in at 3 to 5 pounds for a hen and 6 to 9 pounds for a drake. Domestic Mallards weigh about 2 to 2½ pounds, and the more flavorful Moulard can weigh up to 8 pounds. The Moulard is a cross-breed of the Muscovy and Mallard ducks, similar in taste to the Barbarie. They are raised especially for foie gras. Barbarie drakes can weigh anywhere from 5 to 9 pounds, while the hen weighs in at 3 to 5 pounds. Generally speaking, the Barbarie breast is larger than the Long Island, Pekin, or Mallard. All domestic ducks should be plump, have white skin, and smell fresh. Domestic ducks have a less pronounced flavor than wild ducks. The high fat content of some domestic birds makes them particularly suitable for roasting. While the fat keeps the meat moist, it also can make the bird greasy. Pricking the skin before cooking and while the duck roasts is essential so that the fat can drain as the bird cooks.

There are over one hundred varieties of wild duck, but in the United States we see only a few types of this waterfowl on the table. Canvasback, teal, Mallard, black duck, butterball, and spoonback are some of the more popular ducks, while gadwall, pintail, baldplate, shoveller, wood duck, American golden-eye, and common eider are some of the lesser-known types. Wild ducks tend to weigh less than the domestic varieties, but they make up for their small size with more flavor. Some wild ducks may have a slightly fishy taste due to their diet. This can be remedied by stuffing them with citrus fruits, onions, or herbs, or by soaking the bird overnight in milk or buttermilk. Wild ducks have less fat than domestic, which makes barding or larding necessary in most cases. Check under the skin to see how thick the layer of fat is. Roasting or braising is suitable for wild duck. It is best to serve roasted birds medium rare, or slightly pink, to showcase its gamey flavor. Domestic duck, on the other hand, is usually served well done.

Smoked duck is one of the best smoked fowl products available. It can be purchased whole or cut into breast sections, but either way you will be in for a real treat. The meat from the whole bird is a bit more stringy and chewy than the breast meat alone. Alder and apple wood are typically used for the cold-smoking process.

FREE-RANGE CHICKEN

Chicken has been domesticated all over the world for centuries. All chickens were once raised to have free run of the range, and ate a diet consisting of natural food. Today chickens are raised in pens with little or no natural light and are fed chemicals. This results in birds with little texture or flavor. The recent trend toward organically fed free-range chicken is resulting in an excellent, safe-to-eat product. Free-range chickens taste better and have a firmer texture. Their flavor is similar to that of a pheasant or capon. Many natural foods stores, good grocery stores, and specialty meat markets offer free-range chickens. Because this chicken is more juicy and tender, it requires less cooking time than a pen-raised chicken of the same weight. Free-range chickens are generally a bit smaller than their chemically fed counterparts and have less fat. They can be used in all chicken recipes, and used in place of pheasant in most recipes.

GOOSE

Goose is similar to duck in bone structure and fat content. Goose has long been a traditional favorite for holiday celebrations. The recent decline in its popularity in this country is due in part to the high fat content of this tasty fowl. The knowledgeable cook, however, can prepare a goose without excessive fat or grease. If cooked properly, the meat will be very moist and slightly stringy. Roast a goose as you would a duck, pricking the skin from time to time with a sharp fork to release the fat. The skin should be golden brown and crisp.

A domestic goose can weigh from 8 to 12 pounds, depending on the variety and age; it should not be over one year of age. Wild geese such as the Canadian, the white-fronted goose, and the snow or blue goose tend to have less fat and are generally smaller and less tender. Geese have a very large breastbone and a large frame. These, combined with their high fat content, cause them to yield a smaller amount of meat than their size suggests. The meat is dark and has a robust flavor.

GUINEA FOWL

This bird is originally from Africa, but it has been enjoyed throughout Europe for centuries. The Portuguese started to import large quantities from West Africa in the sixteenth century and the bird has been popular ever since. They are still found in the wild but are also raised under free-range conditions.

Also called a Guinea hen, this pheasantlike bird has white and dark meat that is at once chewy and moist, and the dark meat is particularly dense and rich in flavor. A young Guinea fowl weighs about 1 pound, while the adult version can weigh between 2 and 3 pounds. The frame is rather large, so the percentage of meat per pound is a bit less than you might expect. The bird is also quite lean, so barding is essential when roasting. The smaller sizes should be marinated and then grilled or broiled. The larger birds may be roasted, braised, or used in a stew.

PARTRIDGE

Wild partridge, such as blue grouse and drummer partridge, are found throughout the United States, and farm-raised birds are available year round. Partridge was originally introduced to the United States from Europe, but now game farms abound with this favored bird, which has plump legs and distinctive plumage. The chukar partridge, the most common domesticated type, has light meat and can weigh over a pound. The French partridge, similar to the quail, usually weighs about 9 ounces. Some varieties, such as the Scottish red-legged partridge, can have a pronounced flavor, dense meat, and a chewy texture. All partridge is lean and must be roasted with fat covering the breast. It can also be marinated and grilled or braised. Some partridge varieties may be called grouse or quail.

PHEASANT

The pheasant is one of the most popular and mild tasting of the game birds. It is similar to chicken in texture, size, and flavor. This wonderful bird is commercially raised in California and Pennsylvania, and on smaller farms found throughout the United States. "Semi-wild" pheasants are raised in controlled hunting areas in the United States but are sold mostly to restaurants. Originally from Asia, wild pheasant is found in the northern states and in parts of Europe. Gamekeepers raise pheasant in England, where shooting for sport and for the table has been popular for generations. The wild bird has a more pronounced flavor than the domesticated.

Pheasant is marketed in three different sizes: baby, adult, and mature. The baby pheasant usually weighs about 1 pound and has tender meat. An adult pheasant weighs 2 to 2½ pounds, and the mature version can be 2 to 3½ pounds. Young pheas-

ants have short, rounded claws, while older birds tend to have long, pointed ones. The baby and adult are excellent grilled or roasted, while the mature pheasant is best braised or used in a stew. Many wild pheasants are extra lean and require barding if cooked by a dry-heat method. The meat is similar to free-range chicken but has a more pronounced taste and a chewier texture. The baby or adult pheasant is preferred because the meat is more tender. The skin should be firm and a young bird should have a flexible breastbone. Free-range chicken can be substituted for pheasant in most recipes.

POUSSIN

A chicken under the age of 4 weeks, this rather plump bird is prized for its tender and juicy flesh. It is quite delicate in flavor and texture, but has a larger breast than a full-grown chicken. They usually weigh about 1 pound each and have a fairly large percent of meat for the frame. Poussin is perfect for grilling, broiling, or roasting. The breastbone should be flexible and the skin smooth.

QUAIL

The wild quail is a migratory bird hunted in early autumn. They are also raised for the table. Quail is one of the smallest and most delicate game fowl in the United States or Europe. Hunters usually look for the native white-meat bobwhite variety found in Texas and some Eastern states. The crested, California, valley, and mountain quail can all be found in California. The Courternix, raised mostly on farms in South Carolina and Georgia, has dark flesh and is particularly tasty. The weight differs depending on the variety and age of the bird, but most quail weigh 5 to

6 ounces. When properly cooked, the skin turns golden brown and crispy, rendering the flesh tender and slightly chewy in texture. Because quail are so small and lean it is necessary to marinate them or bard them with fat. The meat dries out easily, so take care when cooking them. Quail are generally grilled, deep fried, broiled, or pan roasted and are served with the breast meat still pink. Boning these tiny birds is tedious to say the least, but if you can find them already boned they are wonderful stuffed and roasted. Plan on serving at least two quail per person.

RABBIT

Rabbit played a large role in the diet of early Americans. Still plentiful in the United States, it is one of the more common game animals found on the table.

Most good poultry shops carry frying or stewing rabbit, and some supermarkets carry frozen rabbits. The size, weight, and taste of a rabbit depends on its diet, species, and whether it is wild or domestic. Generally speaking, wild rabbits have dark meat and are smaller than farm-raised rabbits, which usually have white meat. Farm-raised rabbits are similar to chicken in flavor, while the texture of their flesh is similar to either pork loin or chicken, depending on the age, size, and cut of the rabbit. Most frying rabbits are about 2 to 3 pounds in weight and stewing rabbits are 5 to 6 pounds. Both have delicious meat and a lot of small bones. A fryer can of course be pan fried, but is also good marinated and then grilled. Rabbit is very lean and should be cooked with enough fat and/or liquid to keep it moist. Stewing rabbits may be sectioned and cooked in a stew or braised. The loin is particularly tasty roasted or broiled.

SNOW GROUSE

This distinctive game bird is held in high esteem by those who know wild fowl. Grouse, which feeds on heather shoots and berries, has a unique dark flesh and a pronounced taste. Black grouse, Coq de Bruyère, or blackcock can be almost as large as a pheasant and have a strong flavor. The more familiar red grouse is small and has a preferred texture and flavor. The British grouse, or willow ptarmigan, and the British ptarmigan, also known as the rock ptarmigan, are the most common varieties in the United States. The dusky grouse can be found in Mexico and the Southern states. Ruffled grouse, prairie chicken, and sage cock are other varieties. Most snow grouse is imported from Sweden, where this wild fowl is popular. Grouse is mostly wild, but some is raised on farms, especially in Europe.

A young grouse has a soft beak and a fragile skull, while an older bird will have a firm beak and a hard skull. Grouse under the age of 6 months are best, and anything older should be braised. A grouse can weigh anywhere from 6 ounces to 1 pound, although they are usually in the 8- to 12-ounce range. The size and weight varies from species to species, but usually one grouse per person is ample. The flesh is similar to red meat. The breast is quite large and the meat is red in color, even after it is cooked. There isn't much fat on grouse, so moist-heat cooking or roasting with fat covering the breast is suggested.

SQUAB

A squab is a young pigeon 4 to 6 weeks old. They are too young to fly because they have not developed all their feathers. As a result, the meat

is particularly delicate and tender. Until recently, these wild birds were only available from hunters. They are now raised on farms, primarily in California.

Squabs weigh anywhere from 12 ounces to 1 pound, and although they are small birds they have quite a bit of meat. The meat is dark, moist, and lean and does not taste particularly gamey. They can be stuffed and roasted whole, or split for grilling or broiling.

VENISON

Venison has been an important part of the American diet for centuries. Deer, elk, reindeer, moose, antelope, and caribou are all called venison. Red deer from New Zealand is one of the more popular varieties of deer and can be purchased wild or domesticated. Roebuck, whitetail, fallow, Sika, and Muntjac deer are some of the other farm-raised or wild species available. Each type has a slightly different flavor, and the fat content can differ greatly from one to another. But for the most part, venison is quite lean and fairly assertive in flavor. The meat, depending on the type, age, and cut, is generally finer in texture and darker in color than beef or lamb. Because most venison is darker than beef and has a distinct lack of marbling, it needs additional fat added in the form of barding or larding during the cooking process. Most large cuts of meat require slow, moist cooking, while the tender steaks and loin can be grilled or roasted.

WILD BOAR

The European wild boar was introduced to the United States in the early 1900s; it is a cross between the Russian boar and the razorback. Native American pigs can be found in South America, Mexico, and parts of the Southwest; they are also raised on farms in some states. Wild boar has a taste and texture similar to domestic pig but is usually chewier, leaner, and has a more pronounced flavor. A traditional European game animal, boar is widely available in the United States but has a very restricted hunting season. Luckily it can be purchased through game outlets. The larger cuts do well with slow, moist cooking methods. Domestic pig can be substituted for wild boar in this book. As with pork, boar can carry trichinae, the bacteria that cause trichinosis, so be sure to cook the meat thoroughly, until no pink is visible; an internal temperature of 150° to 165° is recommended.

WILD TURKEY

Wild turkeys have been re-introduced to several parts of the United States, and are becoming widely available for hunting. Wild turkeys are also raised on game farms, which makes them relatively easy to find all year round. Domestic turkeys can weigh between 12 and 30 pounds, while a wild turkey usually weighs anywhere from 6 to 12 pounds. The wild variety has a larger frame and a bit less meat overall, but it has a larger breast and longer legs than the domestic.

Large turkeys are almost always roasted, but smaller birds may be sectioned and braised or used in a stew. The carcass of a cooked turkey can be used with other uncooked fowl to make a good turkey stock for soup. When roasting a wild turkey it is necessary to bard it (to cover the breast with fat) before cooking, and it is important to baste frequently. Wild turkeys have considerably less fat than the domestic variety and therefore need extra fat and moisture while cooking; their meat is less tender than that of domestic turkeys.

If you have your own smoker you can smoke a turkey breast or a whole turkey. Smoked turkey breast is available in most good grocery stores and specialty meat markets and is a fine commercial product. The two most common smoking processes are categorized by temperature: hot or cold. Hot smoking involves very low but constant heat in combination with smoke from a variety of wood chips. In cold smoking the product is treated only by the smoke created from burning a variety of wood chips; it is not cooked during the process but oftentimes is cooked before smoking. A cold-smoked product is usually milder and less smoky tasting than the hot version. Hot smoking is used when the item to be smoked also needs to be cooked or if it could spoil in the time it takes to cold smoke it. Because a whole turkey is so large, a hot-smoking process is used instead of a cold process. The heat cooks the meat as the alder wood smokes it, and the results are delicious. Hot smoking is generally done at home in special smokers or grills that are adapted to smoking, while cold smoking is usually done in a commercial smokehouse.

BASICS

COOKING TECHNIQUES

Cooking methods for game are basically the same as for domestic animals; the one primary difference between them is the fat content of game. When animals run free in the wild they generally develop more muscle and have less fat. This not only affects the taste of the meat, but also changes the bones, fiber, tissue, and skin of the animal. Added fat must be used in many cases to prevent the flesh from drying out. Marinating, proper cooking, or sauces do not necessarily ensure juicy meat. Larding and barding, two traditional methods for adding fat to meat, will be discussed in more detail in the following notes.

In addition to the basic techniques for game I have included a few general cooking guidelines. These simple steps will help you use this book and will make cooking more relaxing and enjoyable.

Cooking game is not complicated or difficult. In most cases the pronounced flavor of the rich meat serves as the focus of a meal, so most recipes in this book are based on simple preparations. The majority of these menus use familiar ingredients and traditional cooking techniques.

Cooking Mushrooms: Always use a small amount of fat and a large pan when cooking mushrooms. Most mushrooms are very sturdy and contain a high percentage of water. They should be cooked over high heat, which will free them of their water and render the mushrooms meaty and firm rather than mushy and limp. Never crowd mushrooms, or they will steam instead of sear, which makes for mushy, bland-tasting mushrooms. Stir frequently, until they are golden brown and dry.

Dressing Salads: To make the best possible green salad, first wash and dry the greens *thoroughly*. Wet greens make for a limp and tasteless salad, as the dressing will not adhere, and the greens will lie in a wet heap on the plate. Second, dress the greens just before serving and add only as much dressing or vinaigrette as necessary. Overdressing the greens will also make the salad limp and wet. Use a large bowl for mixing, and arrange the greens on the plates so they are fluffy, rather than flat. Add croutons or nuts at the last minute or as a garnish, as they will most likely get soggy if added directly to the greens. The recipes for dressings in this book make ¾ cup to 1 cup. Do not use the entire recipe for a salad for 4 or even 8. Use only as much as needed (1 to 2 tablespoons per person) and store the remaining dressing in the refrigerator.

Making Vinaigrettes or Marinades: With proper mixing, dressings and marinades can be smooth emulsions instead of separate mixes of fat and acid (oil and vinegar). An emulsion tastes better, because the ingredients are held in suspension, distributing the flavors throughout the liquid. This allows vegetables, greens, pasta, rice, or meat to receive a portion of every ingredient used in the dressing.

To make a vinaigrette: Place the oil (and garlic or mustard, if used in the recipe) in a bowl and whisk for 1 minute. Slowly add the vinegar, whisking all the while, watching to see that as you add the vinegar, the whisking action is strong enough and fast enough to incorporate the acid into the oil. When all the vinegar has been used you may add the remaining ingredients. Because most vinaigrettes will separate at room temperature, they should be stored in the refrigerator until ready for use. Follow the same procedure for marinades. Chances are the liquid portion of the recipe is wine or a combination of wine and vinegar. Do not use a blender or food processor to make vinaigrettes. These machines are fine for mayonnaise, if used on very slow speed, but they are too violent for more delicate emulsions.

Marinating Foods: Marinating does two things to food: it adds flavor and it tenderizes. Generally speaking, the strength of the ingredients and the length of time the food is marinated affects the intensity of the food's flavor. The acid in a marinade tenderizes; fats add moisture and keep food from sticking to cooking surfaces; and herbs, spices, and other flavoring agents add flavor. The acid can be in the form of vinegar, citrus juice, wine, or tomato products. Usually olive oil is used for the fat, and appropriate herbs, spices and/or minced garlic, ginger, or onion can be used for additional flavoring. Always try to cover the food completely with the marinade. A heavy, self-sealing plastic bag is good for this. Larger, thicker pieces of food require longer marinating, as do tough cuts of meat or poultry.

Marinate food in the refrigerator unless you are pressed for time, in which case you can marinate food at room temperature for 1 or 2 hours. It is important to turn the food in the marinade so that all sides have contact with the liquid; turn at least once every 3 hours if possible. Use an acid-free container such as stainless steel, glass, non-porous ceramic, or plastic so that the acids in the marinade do not interact with the vessel; do not use untreated aluminum or uncoated cast iron. Many recipes in this book use marinades and require 1 or 2 days for marinating. This time period is preferred because the flavors will have more time to penetrate and the food will become more tender. If food has been refrigerated, be sure to bring it to room temperature before cooking.

Rendering Fat: Fatty birds such as duck, goose, and most non-free-range chickens have soft, yellow fat around and under the outer skin. Remove this before cooking and save it for rendering. To render the fat, place the chunks of fat in a saucepan and heat slowly. When the fat has completely melted, pour it into a clean, dry jar and store in the refrigerator. This will keep for 2 to 3 months. Use the fat for sautéing vegetables, in grain dishes, or for sauces and soups. Each variety of fat has a distinct taste and adds depth and flavor to any dish you use it in. Use part fat and part olive oil if you are worried about saturated fat intake.

To Toast Nuts: Preheat the oven to 350°. Spread the nuts on a dry baking sheet and bake for 5 to 10 minutes, depending on what kind of nut you are toasting. Pine nuts take the least amount of time, and can go from light brown to burned black in seconds! Watch all nuts carefully, as their age and water content, along with the weather, will affect the length of time necessary for proper toasting. The nuts are done when they turn golden or toasty brown and their aroma fills the air.

To Skin Hazelnuts: Place the nuts in a single layer on an ungreased baking pan. Toast in a preheated 350° oven for 10 to 12 minutes, or until the skin starts to blister. Remove the nuts from oven and wrap them in a kitchen towel. Rub the nuts in the towel to remove the skins. Or place the toasted nuts in a large fine sieve and rub them against the sides of the sieve, using a towel. Allow the nuts to cool before storing them in an airtight container.

To Roast Peppers: Buy firm peppers for roasting. Using tongs or a long fork, hold a pepper over a gas flame, rotating it as the skin turns black. When all sides, top, and bottom are black, place the pepper in a plastic or paper bag and seal. Steam the peppers for at least 30 minutes, then rub off the black skin and remove the seeds and core. To grill peppers, follow the same technique as for a gas flame. To oven roast peppers, preheat the oven to 500°. Place the peppers on a sheet pan and cook until the skin starts to wrinkle or turn brown. Rotate to ensure even cooking. To store roasted peppers, place them in a jar and cover them with olive oil or a mixture of oil and vinegar and a few cloves of garlic. Cover and store in the refrigerator for 1 to 2 months.

To Slice Soft Cheeses: Refrigerate the cheese for at least 2 hours. Using a serrated knife, cut the cheese gently and slowly, using a sawing motion.

To Sliver Vegetables: Carrots, zucchini, cucumber, potatoes, and any other root vegetables can be slivered by hand. This cut differs from a julienne cut in that the ends are tapered rather than blunt and the slice is thinner and usually longer. Make a diagonal cut across the vegetable. Stack the slices and cut into long skinny pieces about ⅛ inch across and however long the slice is, usually about 1 to 1½ inches.

To Wash Greens: Fill the sink with clean, cold water. Submerge the greens and wash them gently in the water. Remove the greens and dry thoroughly in a spinner or between clean, dry, lint-free towels. If the greens are very dirty or sandy, wash a second time in clean water. Do not drain the water out of the sink and *then* remove the greens; the sand and dirt will stick to the greens and they will have to be washed all over again.

STORAGE AND HANDLING

Fresh fowl are extremely perishable. They should be stored at refrigerator temperatures between 32° and 40°. Do not use after 3 days, and never refreeze thawed poultry or wild fowl. Store in loosely wrapped plastic or place on a roasting rack if you plan to cook it within 6 or 8 hours. Whole birds are less perishable than cut-up birds, so keep this in mind when purchasing and storing the various types of fowl.

Thaw a frozen bird in the refrigerator for 1 to 2 days for a 4- to 5-pound bird and 2 to 3 days for larger fowl. If you are pressed for time you can thaw the bird under cold running water in its original wrapper. Try to cook the bird as soon as it has completely thawed.

Use a clean, dry cutting board for handling fowl. When finished, wash the board with hot water and soap to prevent cross-contamination. Wash all utensils and your hands accordingly.

Game meats are similar to beef, lamb, and pork and require little in the way of special handling. Assuming the meat has been well aged, all that is required is proper storage until it is ready to use. Store meat in loosely wrapped plastic or butcher paper in the refrigerator between 32° and 40°. If you cannot use the meat within 2 or 3 days, you should freeze it. Wrap the meat tightly in butcher paper and cover with foil. Be sure to label with the type and cut of meat and the date.

TIMING

Timing is affected by many variables. The temperature of the oven or grill; the age, size, and type of game; whether or not the game was marinated first and for how long; the temperature of the meat before cooking; how long the oven was preheated; whether the meat was fresh or had been frozen—all play an important role. Use the times in these recipes as basic guidelines, but please be aware of these variables when timing your meal. I do not like to use a thermometer; I think it is safer and wiser to learn to "read" the food, instead of a gauge with numbers.

Until recently, most fowl has usually been cooked well done. The current restaurant trend of serving poultry and wild fowl medium rare is not appealing to me. Dried-out and overcooked fowl, however, is not appealing either. Traditionally, wild duck and a few other wild birds such as grouse, quail, and partridge are served with the meat slightly pink. Domesticated fowl can be a carrier of salmonella bacteria, which is killed when the meat is cooked just until no longer pink. Wild fowl may carry other diseases, so be sure to purchase all game from a reputable dealer whom you trust. Cooking *anything* requires practice and a general awareness of food and how it reacts to heat. With a little sensitivity and some general guidelines you should be able to cook your choice of wild fowl or game perfectly.

Generally speaking, birds 1 pound and under require 10 to 15 minutes of cooking per pound; 4- to 6-pound birds require 15 to 20 minutes per pound; and you can count on roughly 20 minutes per pound for larger birds. Another test is to prick the underside or thigh of the bird with a fork to see if the juices run clear. If the juices are still red or pink, it means the meat is probably still red or pink. Wiggling the leg of a bird to check for doneness can be misleading, as it could indicate tender, well-done dark meat and dry, overcooked white meat. This test is best used in conjunction with the two aforementioned guidelines. Some young birds, such as Guinea fowl, squab, and poussin, have pink bones and slightly reddish or pink meat next to the bone; this does not mean the meat is not done.

Game animals such as venison, buffalo, and wild boar come in a variety of cuts, sizes, and shapes. The cooking method and the age, size, and cut of meat will dictate the amount of time required to achieve the proper doneness. New York steaks, loin, and strip loin are tender cuts that are usually roasted, grilled, or broiled, while the tougher cuts of meat like the shoulder and leg are cooked using slow moist-heat cooking methods. These tougher cuts of meat are done when they are tender, soft, and pliable. Boar and wild pig must be cooked until no longer pink, but the tender cuts of other game meats are cooked to degrees of doneness just as a steak from a steer would be: rare, medium rare, medium, medium well, and well done. The flavors of venison, buffalo, and bear are more pronounced when the meat is served rare or medium rare, but if your family or guests prefer their meat cooked longer, then please do so. Most passionate meat-eaters prefer their steaks cooked rare or at most, medium rare. I prefer my meat cooked medium rare, but when cooking for friends or customers I simply cook the meat according to their wishes.

GENERAL COOKING TERMS

Baste: *Basting* is simply moistening the surface of the meat with liquid or fat while it is cooking. Both add moisture, fat makes the skin golden brown. (Goose and duck do not need any basting, as they are very fatty birds.) Basting is generally done every 25 to 30 minutes for larger birds, and every 15 minutes for smaller birds if the total cooking time is less than 1½ hours. More frequent basting allows too much heat to escape from the oven and affects the cooking in an adverse way. Basting is not necessary when the bird is placed breast-side down, except during the last half hour, when the breast is turned right side up for browning. A bulb baster is the easiest to use, but a spoon will do just fine.

Blanch: To *blanch* is to partially cook an item in boiling water or fat. Usually the item will be cooked again, using a different cooking method, although sometimes nuts and fruits are blanched so that the skin is more easily removed. To blanch: Bring a large pot of salted water to a boil. Add the food and cook to the desired state of doneness—this will vary depending on the food and how it will be used later. Remove the food from the water and drain in a colander. If you are blanching vegetables, then place the blanched food in ice water for approximately 10 minutes. This stops the cooking action, keeps the vegetables crisp, and helps to retain the bright colors. When blanching potatoes, however, do not rinse or cool in ice water, as they will become mushy and break apart more easily. Salt in the blanching water brings out the flavor of foods and helps to retain the color of green and orange vegetables. If you are blanching salt pork, however, additional salt is not necessary.

Braise: To *braise* means to cook food covered in a small amount of liquid and fat over a long period of time using relatively low heat. Usually the item is browned first in a small amount of fat. This sears in the flavors and adds an attractive color to the food. This moist-heat cooking method is good for tough or lean meat or poultry and even some root or fibrous vegetables. Braising requires little attention and ensures uniform cooking.

Broil: This dry, radiant-heat cooking method is used to cook tender cuts of meat and poultry quickly. Always preheat the broiler unit of your oven for at least 15 minutes before you intend to use it. A light coating of fat is usually applied to the food just before broiling. The average distance between the food and the heat source is anywhere from 1 to 3 inches. Place larger, thicker pieces of food farther away from the heat and thinner pieces closer. The closer the food is to the heat source or flame, the faster it cooks and the faster the exterior will brown.

Griddle: A *griddle* is a solid, flat cooking surface used primarily for cooking eggs, meat, pancakes, and hash browns. The surface provides steady, even heat and is much cooler than a grill. A large, heavy sauté pan or skillet is a fairly good substitute. A small amount of fat is necessary in either case.

Grill: Technically, to *grill* is to cook food on a metal rack using radiant heat; in this book *grilling* refers to cooking on an outdoor grill. Charcoal, wood, a combination of both, gas, and electricity are the most common sources of heat. Grilling is a dry-heat cooking method and can be used for most small and medium birds, certain cuts of meat, and many vegetables. It is usually a good idea to marinate items to be grilled, as this cooking method does not supply any moisture. All foods should be coated with fat or oil before placing on the rack. It is best to clean the rack with a wire brush before you start the fire. Be sure to let the rack get hot before you place the food on the surface. Depending on the heat from the fire, it will take 5 to 10 minutes to heat the rack thoroughly.

Red-hot coals are glowing red with small flames here and there, and a light layer of gray ash. Slow coals have a thick layer of gray ash, with almost no red showing through. Most recipes call for medium-hot coals, which have a layer of gray ash with a red glow showing through. At this stage, you can hold your hand over the coals at a distance of 6 inches, for 5 to 6 seconds without discomfort. Generally it will take about 45 minutes to get the coals to this stage from the time they are first lit.

Roast: Roasting and baking are dry-heat cooking methods. *Roasting* applies to meat and fowl and *baking* usually refers to breads, pastries, cookies, fish, and vegetables. Roasted and baked foods are cooked uncovered; covering the food changes the process to steaming, a moist-heat cooking method. A roasting rack keeps the food elevated so that the air and heat can circulate around the entire product, producing an evenly cooked bird or piece of meat. When roasting small or medium-sized birds or loins of meat I like to use a flat roasting rack. This increases the flow of heat around the product, making for more even cooking and browning. Use a V-shaped rack for larger birds such as goose, duck, turkey, or capon, or for large cuts of meat. It is always wise to place the rack in a greased baking pan that is larger than the actual rack and the item to be roasted. I suggest greasing the pan as a general rule, because you cannot always predict how much fat will drip from the meat or how fast. Greasing the pan prevents the pan and the drippings from burning while the food cooks.

When roasting a fatty bird such as a duck or goose, always prick the skin just to the meat; do not pierce the meat. Prick the skin before roasting and several times during the cooking time. This releases extra fat from the skin, making the skin crisper and leaner and leaving the meat juicy and moist. Basting is not necessary with fatty birds.

When roasting some whole birds, the legs may take longer to cook than the breasts. Dark meat contains more fat and cooks at a slower rate than white meat, while the lack of fat in the breast meat may make it too dry. Basting with the fat from the bird or added rendered fat will add moisture and flavor. Barding, or covering the breast with a layer of fat, helps to prevent the breast from drying out and adds a pleasant smoky flavor if bacon or pancetta is used. Some cooks like to roast larger birds (3½ pounds or more) such as duck, chicken, capon, and turkey breast-side down for at least half of the cooking time; I prefer to roast larger birds breast-side down until the last half hour of cooking time. The last bit of cooking breast-side up allows the skin to brown, while the inverted roasting helps to make the breast meat juicy and tender.

There are different thoughts on whether a constant moderate temperature is better for roasting than starting with a high temperature for a short period of time followed by a lower temperature for the remaining time. The latter method, referred to as "flash roasting," is the one I prefer because I believe it seals in the juices and makes for a more tender, juicy product. Smaller birds may be cooked at higher temperatures for a short time with great success. They must be watched carefully, however, so that they do not dry out. Most of the recipes in this book use the flash-roasting method, but if you prefer the other method, feel free to use it.

Always let roasted foods rest for 10 to 15 minutes before carving or slicing. This makes the meat juicier, and slicing the meat is easier.

Sauté: To *sauté* means to cook quickly in a small amount of fat, usually in a sauté pan or skillet. A sauté pan differs from a skillet in that it has sloped sides. This allows the food to move about quickly and easily as the pan is tossed, using a rolling action from the wrist. Always heat the pan and the fat before adding the food. Do not crowd food because it lowers the temperature too much, which results in steaming instead of searing. Use high heat and keep the food moving either with the motion of the pan or with a spoon. I prefer nonstick surfaces for all pans and especially for sauté pans, as it encourages food to move about quickly and with ease.

Sear: To *sear* is to cook in a very small amount of fat over very high heat. This method is usually used when a medium-rare product is desired.

Preparing Fowl for Cooking

Barding and Larding: Wild fowl tends to be on the lean side, and extra-lean birds such as Guinea hens, partridge, and wild turkey need extra fat to make the meat moist and palatable. Use fatty bacon or salt pork sliced about ¼ inch thick. Place the slices of fat over the breast and legs of the birds and truss. Remove the fat during the last half hour for larger birds, or just before serving in the case of smaller birds. If you use bacon you may want to leave it on the bird, as it can be a tasty addition to the dish if it is crispy and golden brown. Larding is used primarily for lean cuts of meat, but it also can be used for fowl. Pork fat is cut into lardoons, then inserted into the meat with a larding needle. The lardoons should be cut about ⅛ inch in diameter and should be of uniform shape and size. This time-consuming procedure is not necessary for any of the recipes in this book.

To Butterfly: To butterfly a bird, place it breast side down on a cutting board and, using a knife, cut through all the bones on one side of the backbone through to the neck. Split the bird open, cut off the backbone, and save it for stock. Remove the breastbone by slicing it away from the meat. Press on the bird with your hands to make it flat.

To Remove the Fishy Taste from Wild Waterfowl: If a wild duck or goose has been feeding on fish, chances are it will have a fishy taste. This is not offensive to some, but if you prefer your fowl a bit more subtle, soak the bird in milk or buttermilk overnight to remove any fishy taste. You may also stuff the cavity with lemon, orange, lime, and onion and refrigerate the bird overnight. Remove the citrus fruits and onion before cooking.

To Split: Follow the same procedure as for butterflying, but make a final cut through the center of the breast after removing the breastbone so that the bird forms two equal pieces.

To Stuff and Truss: Always stuff the bird just before cooking to prevent the growth of bacteria in the stuffing. Place the stuffing in the cavity of the bird, filling it only three-quarters full and packing loosely. The stuffing will expand during cooking and can leak and even break fragile or smaller birds. Close the openings with string, or with toothpicks in the case of fowl weighing 1 pound or less. If there is a large flap of skin you may use it to close the opening by the neck. Tie the legs together and turn the wings back. Use the same procedure for trussing with or without stuffing.

Preparing Game Meats for Cooking

If the meat has been well aged, there is very little in the way of preparation needed for cooking game meats.

To Remove the Gamey Taste from Meat: If the meat smells too gamey you may soak it in a solution of ½ cup vinegar to 1 gallon water, with the addition of 3 tablespoons of kosher salt, overnight. Usually, however, marinating the meat is enough to tone down a gamey taste.

To Bard and Lard: *Barding* is used when the meat is very lean and would be improved by the addition of extra fat. Bacon, fatback, or salt pork can be tied to the meat before roasting. This will prevent the meat from drying out and will add moisture and flavor. *Larding* is inserting strips of fat into the piece of meat using a larding needle. This adds marbling to what would otherwise be a lean piece of meat. Larding is used with extremely dry cuts of meat. The strips of fat are removed after cooking, just as the fat used in barding is removed.

The more popular cuts of game available through the retailer are so similar to the familiar cuts of beef and pork that no special instructions for cooking are necessary. Larger cuts of meat are good for slow cooking methods, while the smaller, more tender, cuts are great grilled, broiled, or roasted.

WINE
AND
FOOD

WINE AND FOOD

By Brian St. Pierre

Any meal tastes better with wine, although it needs to be the right sort of wine. For many people there's the rub, the same cautionary voice in our heads that reminds us that you can't have roses without thorns, or that if you dance you must pay the piper—the voice of rectitude, the preemptive strike so favored by Puritans and snobs. In fact, wine is a splendid example of pluralism, offering an abundance of "right" choices with which to elevate a meal and make food taste better. The whole business of matching food and wine isn't nearly as complicated or constricted as it often seems, let alone as daunting.

The reasons for this unnecessary insecurity are mostly historical, somewhat cultural, and certainly rooted in the long drought of Prohibition, when from 1919 to 1933 it was illegal to make or take a drink, with few exceptions. Repeal of this ridiculous law came in the depths of the Depression, which gave wine drinkers two choices for the most part, neither easy: domestic jug wine made in a hurry, or relatively expensive imported stuff.

It wasn't until after World War II that Americans began to have a supply of decent, affordable domestic and imported wines and what we now call a lifestyle to fit them into. There was one thing missing, though: a generation's worth of knowledge about the flavors and uses of wine. We were babes in the woods, starting from scratch, looking for guidance.

In the wine-growing countries of Europe, this would have been a redundant notion; they had no need for wine columns in the newspapers, or the wine books and newsletters that proliferated here. Wine was something you had with most meals, something you grew up with, a good familiar creature. Matching food and wine was easy: you drank the local stuff. A rabbit would be washed down with Riesling in Alsace or Barolo in the Piedmont; in a Paris bistro, the choice might depend on where the chef or owner was born and raised. The average Italian or Frenchman regarded "rules" about matching food and wine the way he regarded the tax laws, with amused disdain.

In the nineteenth century, given our frontier mentality and waves of immigration from Mediterranean countries, things were looser and easier here; anything went. The shock of World War I and Prohibition brought us back

closer to our puritanical beginnings, and though we shook off some of its effects, we've never been quite the same. In a sense, we went from a casual, shirtsleeve acceptance of the amiable sensuality of wine to a buttoned-up, formal, Anglo-Saxon approach; the gentility of England had become our model.

Wine runs all through British novels and plays, essays and poems, in Dickens and Wilde, Thackeray and Byron, on to the drawing-room and manor-house comedies of Evelyn Waugh, Noel Coward, and P. G. Wodehouse, the mysteries of Agatha Christie and Dorothy Sayers, and flows liberally in "Upstairs, Downstairs." Also, though the British made no wine of their own, they have always been superb merchants of it, inventing port, marrying into the old sherry families, and selling Bordeaux all over the world; as a result they became known as great connoisseurs.

As their judgements filtered through to us, more often than not in bits and pieces, something got lost in the translation. It wasn't necessarily the fault of the sender: What we missed was that we were often getting the ritualized, stratified, codified conventional wisdom of the upper classes and landed gentry, the people with the money and space to build wine cellars and maintain large household staffs, with grand dinners as a major form of entertainment (and source of prestige). Their self-confidence, often to the point of arrogance, was reassuring.

We had, basically, gotten the words but not the music. I can remember, as a boy, seeing a neighbor we thought to be terribly sophisticated solemnly pouring Italian Swiss Colony ruby port from a gallon jug into a decanter; never mind that the wine would never throw a sediment and didn't need decanting (indeed, it wasn't even true port)— that was the way it was done. Another time, with a celebratory rack of lamb, we splurged on a four-year-old bottle of Château Lafite, twenty years away from its prime, rough and raw, and none of us would admit that we couldn't stand it—we were, after all, Doing the Right Thing.

Our little knowledge had ossified into a conservative conventional wisdom, based on a simple catechism: Red with meat. White with fish. Rosé with ham, or as a compromise between red and white. After a while, when we knew more, the "rules" were refined: Cabernet Sauvignon with lamb. Pinot Noir with roast beef. Chardonnay with shellfish. Riesling and other lighter whites with chicken. Useful enough generalizations that could get you through many a dinner reasonably well, but perhaps not superbly. Like twin beds, instant coffee, frozen carrots,

and television news, they're just not quite sufficient.

Happily, we've come a long way in the last two decades. The wine business all over the world has evolved faster than any of us can keep up with, and America leads the world in the amount and number of wines we import, giving us a wide variety of choices—and superb opportunities: Chardonnay from California, France, or Australia; Riesling from Washington, Alsace, or the Rheingau; Barolo, Barbaresco, and Dolcetto from northern Italy. The Chianti we drink is robust and flavorful now, and unlike the thin, raspy Chiantis we drank in college, they don't come in straw-wrapped bottles suitable for reuse as candleholders.

And we have begun to take the measure of this bounty, relaxing and learning to go with our instincts when it comes to wine. We may be moving tentatively and still somewhat conservatively, but we are getting somewhere, drinking Pinot Noir with salmon, Zinfandel with chicken, Sauvignon Blanc or Pinot Grigio with pork chops, and Riesling with veal cutlets, mixing and matching to achieve something closer to maximum flavor than before.

In this, we have been greatly helped by a new breed of chefs, cheerfully reinventing the way we eat: Bocuse, Blanc, Verge, Guerard, and the brothers Troisgros in France, with their brilliant inspirations of nouvelle cuisine; Alice Waters and Jeremiah Tower in Berkeley, with their inspired simplicity of what has come to be called California cuisine; Bradley Ogden and Larry Forgione recreating American cooking; Barbara Tropp and Ken Hom redefining Chinese food; and the thousands of others who have followed, to the point where it seems at times that the global village has a communal kitchen.

The wine cellar has been shared, too, and nicely sensual explorations of food and wine have gone along in tandem. And as the boundaries have widened, game has returned to the table, no longer an exotic rarity for the adventuresome or a reward for the sure shot. With all the added flavors of cross-ethnic spices and herbs, the new vegetables, and the sauces reduced to their essences that now prevail, it was only logical to apply them to game, with its similar directness and robust taste, freeing us all from the burden of fussy, elaborate preparations and syrupy, domineering sauces.

It's less a new approach than a return to a fine old one, of course, and its straightforwardness provides a nice opportunity for the same sort of straight-on openness to wine, embracing the myriad choices available here and now.

The small universe of game immediately changes some of our perceptions: A few of its furred members are white-meated, while several of its feathered ones are dark-meated; some of the apparently plump meats are in fact lean, and require marinating or moist heat, such as braising. Above all, the flavors are direct, and so should be the flavors of the appropriate wines. Just as the best sauce enhances a meat by underscoring its flavor without overpowering it, wine should create further harmony, balancing out the meal.

Chardonnay, for example, is often characterized by a clean, tart taste likened to the tang of green apples, while the oak barrels most of them age in add a distinctive undertone which for me makes a perfect fit with dishes like Roast Pheasant with Sun-dried Tomatoes or Smoked Duck and Goose Ravioli; the pleasant acidity of a balanced Chardonnay refreshingly plays off the richness of the foods, while its full body and flavor complement them.

Sauvignon Blanc and Alsatian Riesling or Gewürztraminer tend toward lighter body, but are notably spicy wines. Sauvignon (also known as Fumé) Blanc has a fresh-herbal aspect that I think dovetails nicely with Braised Rabbit with Fennel, Olives and Oranges, while Alsatian Riesling, which is notably dry but has a floral aroma, mates well with the more delicate texture and flavor of Braised Pheasant with Sour Cream and Grapes. Alsatian Gewürztraminer, bone-dry and thoroughly spicy, fits right in with a dish like Warm Red Cabbage Salad with Smoked Duck, which presents a mélange of flavors tending toward spiciness.

Among red wines, Pinot Noir is perhaps the best all-around wine for food, relatively light but with a great complexity and depth to its flavor, and a velvet-smooth texture, all of which suit it nicely to Grilled Quail with Honey-Hazelnut Sauce, and Smoked Turkey Tostadas, and make it a worthy backup choice for many other game dishes if your taste doesn't run to heavier reds, and as long as the accompanying sauces aren't too assertive.

Cabernet Sauvignon, the great red wine of Bordeaux and California (and, increasingly, of Australia and Washington) is distinctive, complex, full-bodied, and aggressive with astringent tannin when young; with time—five or six years at least, and more would be better in most cases, especially in that of Bordeaux—the wines soften, become more accessible. Although the flavor isn't the same, the aging curve for Barolo, Italy's greatest red, is, and I have found that either wine goes as well with, for example, Roast Goose with Red Pepper Sauce. On the other hand, I think Cabernet works slightly better with Roast Squab with Balsamic-Port Glaze, and Barolo with

My first choice need not be yours, of course; like all sensual pleasures, wine is highly subjective, as well it should be. If you prefer a dry Riesling or Gewürztraminer with your goose, then that's what you should have, as many Alsatians would; if you're daffy about Pinot Noir or red Burgundy, as many people are, then gladly let it predominate your table. I once met a man who drinks nothing but Dom Perignon, before, during, and after meals, the most delightful example I know of ignorance really being bliss; he doesn't care what I think, and he has that right.

Above all, the most important thing about wine is not to do without it. Colette, so wise in so many things, put it best: "Away from the meal table, you have the pump, the faucet, the spring, and the filter at your disposal. Water is for quenching the thirst. Wine, according to its quality and the soil where it was grown, is a necessary tonic, a luxury, and a fitting tribute to good food. . . . The vine and the wine it produces are two great mysteries. Alone in the vegetable kingdom, the vine makes the true savor of the earth intelligible to man. With what fidelity it makes the translation!"

Venison Stew with Wild Rice and Dried Apricots, but I wouldn't argue with anyone who turned those pairings around, nor turn down an invitation to such a dinner.

Merlot is a somewhat softer wine than these, readier to drink at an earlier age, but still complex and solid enough to fare well with Five-Spice Roast Duck. On the other hand, the earthiness of Chianti Classico seems to strike the best note with Braised Rosemary Partridge with Lentils.

Zinfandel, a wine unique to California, acclaimed for its fresh fruitiness, rich berry character, and easy accessibility, is a good choice for Roast Wild Turkey with Cranberry-Apricot Glaze, which seems to me a similarly amiable dish, as is Grilled Rabbit with Prune-Cognac Sauce; Dolcetto, also a nicely fruity red wine from Italy's Piedmont region, is a good alternative to Zinfandel, and would be my first choice with Roast Poussin with Walnut–Goat Cheese Pasta.

MARINADES, SAUCES, STUFFINGS, AND STOCKS

MARINADES, SAUCES, STUFFINGS, AND STOCKS

MARINADES

To marinate means to soak food in a flavored and seasoned liquid for an extended period of time, usually 6 to 8 hours or overnight, depending on the ingredients in the marinade as well as the kind of food being marinated. The following recipes for marinades are based on a variety of ingredients that will lend an ethnic flavor not only to the marinated food, but also to the entire menu.

Lime and Ancho Pepper Marinade

Latin ingredients make this marinade spicy, thick, and robust.

Makes about 2 cups

4 dried ancho peppers, soaked in water to cover overnight
1 tomato, chopped
4 garlic cloves
1 cup olive oil
⅓ cup fresh lime juice
1 teaspoon ground black pepper

Drain, stem, and seed the soaked ancho peppers. Place the peppers and the remaining ingredients in a blender or food processor and puree until smooth. Store in the refrigerator in a covered container for up to 2 weeks.

Lemon-Rosemary Marinade

Lemon zest or the juice from 1 orange may be added to this marinade for extra flavor.

Makes about 2 cups

1½ cups olive oil
4 tablespoons Dijon mustard
½ cup fresh lemon juice
6 garlic cloves, minced
¼ cup chopped fresh rosemary, or 2 tablespoons crumbled dried rosemary
2 teaspoons ground black pepper

Combine the oil and mustard in a small bowl, whisking to form an emulsion. Add the remaining ingredients and mix well. Store in a covered container in the refrigerator for up to 2 weeks.

Gin Marinade

Gin is the traditional liquor used to temper excessive gamey tastes in game meats and fowl. It leaves an unusual sweet and fruity aftertaste that is particularly pleasant when the meat has a pronounced flavor.

Makes 2¼ cups

1½ cups olive oil
3 tablespoons orange marmalade
3 garlic cloves, minced
1 tablespoon dried basil
1 teaspoon ground black pepper
½ cup gin

Combine the olive oil, marmalade, garlic, basil, and black pepper in a small bowl. Slowly add the gin, whisking all the while with a wire whisk. Store in a covered container in the refrigerator for up to 2 weeks.

Pomegranate Marinade

Use a high-quality imported walnut oil for this marinade. If only milder domestic varieties are available, omit the olive oil and use only walnut oil. If pomegranates are unavailable, substitute bottled pomegranate juice or, as a last resort, frozen cranberry juice concentrate. Bottled pomegranate juice can be found at Middle Eastern markets, specialty markets, and some natural foods stores.

Makes about 2 cups

½ cup walnut oil
1 cup olive oil
2 garlic cloves, minced
1 teaspoon ground black pepper
¼ cup minced fresh parsley
½ cup pomegranate juice or cranberry concentrate

Combine the above ingredients in a small bowl; mix well. Store in a covered container in the refrigerator for up to 2 weeks.

Note: To extract juice from a pomegranate: Slice the fruit in half across the middle. Squeeze with one hand, forcing the seeds and juice from the center of the fruit. Strain through a fine wire mesh.

Red Wine Marinade

This basic marinade is good for most red meat and the more flavorful wild birds. Use a green- or gold-colored extra-virgin olive oil for this recipe.

Makes 2¼ cups

1½ cups fruity olive oil
3 garlic cloves, minced
¾ cup dry red wine
1 teaspoon ground black pepper

Place the olive oil and garlic in a small bowl. Slowly add the red wine, whisking all the while with a wire whisk to form an emulsion. Add the pepper; mix well. Store in a covered container in the refrigerator for up to 2 weeks.

SAUCES

Sauces add flavor, color, and texture to foods, but they should not overpower the flavor of the dish itself. Sauces complement foods, but they cannot mask an improperly cooked dish, nor can they rescue a dry, overcooked piece of meat or fowl. The following sauces are versatile, simple, and straightforward.

Honey-Hazelnut Sauce

Although I usually prefer butter for thickening sauces, I think cornstarch works better in this recipe. A small amount of butter is used at the end to finish the sauce, adding flavor and richness.

Makes about ⅔ cup

1¾ cups homemade chicken stock or low-salt canned chicken broth
3 tablespoons dry sherry
1½ teaspoons cornstarch
2 tablespoons unsalted butter
2 teaspoons honey
¼ cup skinned toasted hazelnuts, minced
Salt and pepper to taste

Place the chicken stock in a small sauté pan or skillet. Bring to a boil and cook over high heat until reduced to about ¾ cup. Combine the sherry and cornstarch in a small bowl; mix well.

Add the cornstarch "slurry" to the chicken stock, whisking all the while. Cook the sauce over moderate heat for 2 to 3 minutes. Add the butter and stir until melted. Add the honey and hazelnuts and cook until smooth. Season with salt and pepper and serve hot.

Fire-Prune Dipping Sauce

Dried red pepper flakes add fire and Chinese black rice vinegar adds depth to this sweet and sour Asian sauce.

Makes about 1¼ cups

6 pitted prunes, chopped
½ cup raisins
1 tomato, chopped
1 large red bell pepper, roasted, peeled, and seeded
3 garlic cloves, chopped
½ cup water
2 tablespoons soy sauce
2 tablespoons Chinese black rice vinegar (available in Asian markets) or red wine vinegar
2 teaspoons dried red pepper flakes
Salt and pepper to taste

Place all of the ingredients in a medium non-aluminum saucepan. Bring the mixture to a boil over high heat. Reduce heat and simmer over moderate heat for 20 minutes, stirring frequently. Allow to cool slightly. Transfer to a blender or food processor and puree until smooth. Strain through a fine sieve and return to the saucepan. Thin with a little water or more vinegar, whichever your palate prefers. Serve at room temperature. Store in a covered container in the refrigerator for up to 2 weeks.

Balsamic-Raspberry Sauce

Pleasantly tart, this deep-rose-colored sauce is excellent with grilled or roasted game. The addition of butter makes it silky and rich, while the vinegars add flavor and acidity.

Makes about 1 cup

½ cup raspberries, mashed with a fork
1 cup homemade chicken stock or canned low-salt chicken broth
2 tablespoons balsamic vinegar
1 tablespoon raspberry vinegar
4 tablespoons unsalted butter
Salt and pepper to taste

Place the raspberries and the chicken stock in a small sauté pan or skillet and cook over high heat until the liquid is reduced by half, about 10 to 12 minutes. Strain through a fine sieve, pushing the raspberry juice through with the back of a wooden spoon. Return the sieved mixture to a small saucepan and bring the liquid to a boil. Add the vinegars and cook over high heat for 2 minutes, stirring often. Add the butter 1 tablespoon at a time, stirring all the while. When all the butter has been added, taste for salt and pepper. Serve hot.

Orange Crème Fraîche

Crème fraîche, a sour cultured cream, can be found at natural foods stores and some cheese and specialty food shops. A good-quality sour cream can be substituted.

Makes ¾ cup

¾ cup crème fraîche
Fresh orange juice, if needed
Grated zest from 1 small orange
Pinch *each* ground nutmeg and white pepper

Thin the crème fraîche, if necessary, with a little orange juice to the consistency of heavy cream. Add the zest and spices and serve at room temperature. Store in the refrigerator for up to 2 weeks.

Red Pepper Sauce

This easy-to-make reddish-orange sauce goes well with grilled vegetables or fowl.

Makes about 1½ cups

1 small red onion, cut into medium dice
2 garlic cloves, minced
3 tablespoons olive oil
2 large red bell peppers, cored, seeded, and chopped
1 tomato, chopped
½ teaspoon dried red pepper flakes
½ teaspoon ground coriander
Splash of balsamic vinegar
Salt and pepper to taste
2 tablespoons unsalted butter (optional)

Cook the onion and garlic in the olive oil over moderate heat for 10 to 12 minutes, stirring occasionally. Add the peppers and cook over high heat for 2 minutes. Add the tomato, pepper flakes, coriander, and vinegar and cook over moderate heat for 10 minutes. Cool slightly. Puree in a blender or food processor until smooth. Strain through a fine sieve. Return to the saucepan. Bring to a boil, taste, and adjust the seasoning. Add 2 tablespoons of butter for added richness, if desired. Store in a covered container in the refrigerator for up to 5 days.

Salsa Cruda

A traditional Mexican salsa, this spicy and colorful combination of fresh ingredients can be made as spicy as you like by adding more jalapeño chilies.

Makes about 2½ cups

1 small onion, finely diced
1 or 2 jalapeños, seeded and chopped
3 ripe tomatoes, finely diced
2 tablespoons chopped fresh cilantro
Salt and pepper to taste

Combine all the ingredients in a small glass or ceramic bowl; mix well. Leave at room temperature for up to 6 hours or cover and store in the refrigerator for 3 or 4 days.

Two-Mustard Sauce

Creamy and thick, this sauce is very good with rare venison or buffalo.

Makes about ¾ cup

1½ cups heavy cream
2 garlic cloves, minced
3 tablespoons Dijon mustard
2 tablespoons coarse-grained prepared mustard
Salt and black pepper to taste

Place the cream and garlic in a large saucepan. Bring to a boil over high heat, stirring constantly to prevent the cream from boiling over. When the cream is reduced by about half and is thick enough to coat the back of a spoon, stir in the two mustards and mix well. Taste and adjust the seasoning.

Madeira Sauce

This decidedly rich and buttery sauce, slightly thickened with a bit of tomato paste, is a fine addition to any meat or fowl dish.

Makes ¾ cup

1½ cups homemade chicken or duck stock or canned low-salt chicken broth
2 shallots, chopped
½ cup Madeira
1 tablespoon tomato paste
3 tablespoons unsalted butter
Salt and pepper to taste

Combine the stock and shallots in a small saucepan. Bring to a boil over high heat and boil until reduced to ½ cup. Strain through a fine sieve. Return the strained liquid to the pan. Add the Madeira and boil for 3 minutes, stirring frequently. Add the tomato paste and mix well. Reduce the heat to moderate and add the butter, 1 tablespoon at a time, stirring all the while. Season with salt and pepper. Store in a covered container in the refrigerator for up to 5 days.

Red Pepper–Ancho Sauce

Use dried ancho or pasilla chilies for this sauce. The chipotle chili is a smoked and dried ripe jalapeño and is very fiery! The combination of peppers and maple syrup makes this balanced sauce neither too hot nor too sweet. The chilies and chili powder can be found in Latin American grocery stores.

Makes about 1 cup

2 dried ancho or pasilla chilies, soaked in water to cover overnight
2 large red bell peppers, roasted, seeded, peeled, and chopped
Juice from 2 limes
1 small onion, finely diced
¼ teaspoon ground cinnamon
1 tablespoon ground chipotle chili
1½ tablespoons maple syrup
Salt and pepper to taste

Drain, seed, and stem the ancho chilies. Place all the ingredients except salt and pepper in a blender or food processor and puree until smooth. Transfer the puree to a saucepan and bring to a boil. Reduce the heat to moderately low and simmer, stirring occasionally, for 15 minutes. Adjust the seasoning with salt and pepper. Strain through a fine sieve and return to the pan to heat to serving temperature. Store in a covered container in the refrigerator for up to 1 week.

Prune-Cognac Sauce

Prunes make this sauce thick and slightly sweet and give it a wonderful deep, dark color.

Makes about 1 cup

1 shallot, chopped
3 garlic cloves, chopped
5 pitted prunes, chopped
1⅔ cups homemade chicken stock or canned low-salt chicken broth
3 tablespoons balsamic vinegar
½ cup cognac
Salt and pepper to taste

In a small, heavy saucepan, bring the shallot, garlic, prunes, and chicken stock to a boil. Reduce the heat and cook over moderate heat for 10 minutes. Allow to cool slightly. Transfer the prune mixture to a blender or food processor and puree until smooth. Return the puree to the pan and bring to a boil over high heat. Add the vinegar and cognac and boil for 2 minutes. Reduce the heat to low and cook, stirring occasionally, for 10 minutes. Season with salt and pepper. Store in a covered container in the refrigerator for about 5 days.

Wild Mushroom Sauce

Use dried mushrooms imported from South America instead of Italian porcini if price is a consideration. The South American versions are full flavored and an excellent buy for the money. For fresh mushrooms use shiitake, porcini, cremini, oyster, or Italian field mushrooms. Be sure to rub or brush all the dirt and grit from the fresh mushrooms before cooking.

Makes about 2 cups

3 to 4 ounces dried porcini mushrooms
2 quarts water
¾ cup Madeira
¾ cup (1½ sticks) unsalted butter
1 pound assorted fresh wild and cultivated mushrooms, stemmed and
    thinly sliced
¼ cup tomato paste
Salt and pepper to taste

In a large saucepan over high heat, combine the dried mushrooms and water; cook over high heat for 25 to 30 minutes. Strain through cheesecloth and squeeze the liquid from the mushrooms to extract all the juice. Discard the mushrooms and return the liquid to the pan. Add the Madeira and bring to a boil. Boil until reduced to 1½ to 2 cups.

Meanwhile, melt 5 tablespoons of the butter in a small sauté pan or skillet over moderate heat and sauté the fresh mushrooms until they are tender but not mushy, about 5 minutes. Set aside.

Over moderate heat, add the tomato paste to the reduced mushroom liquid and stir until smooth. Add the remaining butter in pieces and cook over low heat until all the butter melts. Add the sautéed mushrooms and mix well. Season with salt and pepper.

Pumpkin Seed Pesto

Traditional pesto takes a new twist when pumpkin seeds replace pine nuts, and cilantro and parsley are used in place of fresh basil. This is good tossed with hot cooked pasta and as a dip for vegetables.

Makes about 1½ cups

½ cup parsley sprigs
½ cup cilantro leaves
2 garlic cloves
½ cup pumpkin seeds
½ cup olive oil
Juice of 2 limes
Salt and peper to taste
Olive oil to cover

Combine all the ingredients, except the oil to cover, in a blender or food processor and puree until smooth. Pour into a small bowl and cover with a thin layer of oil until ready to use. Store in a covered container in the refrigerator for up to 1 week.

COMPOUND BUTTERS

Compound butter is simply butter with one or more ingredients added. The most common additions are spices, herbs, and garlic, but peppers, mushrooms, sun-dried tomatoes, and nuts can be used as well. Always use unsalted butter, as it has a better flavor and is fresher. Salt can be added if necessary, but the addition of other flavors usually eliminates the need for salt.

Allspice-Mace Butter

Makes about ⅓ cup

5 tablespoons unsalted butter, softened
½ teaspoon *each* ground allspice and ground mace
Pinch of ground coriander and cayenne
Salt and white pepper to taste

Combine all the ingredients in a small bowl; mix well. Store in a covered container in the refrigerator for up to 2 weeks.

Cilantro-Jalapeño Butter

Makes about ⅓ cup

5 tablespoons unsalted butter, softened
1 garlic clove, minced
1 jalapeño chili, seeded, cored, and minced
2 tablespoons chopped fresh cilantro
Salt and pepper to taste

Combine all the ingredients in a small bowl; mix well. Store in a covered container in the refrigerator for up to 2 weeks.

GLAZES

A glaze is a mixture of several ingredients that is spread on food during or after cooking to add flavor, moisture, color, and sheen. The mixture is usually thick enough to stick to the food but thin enough to create an almost translucent effect on the surface.

Cranberry-Apricot Glaze

Makes about 1¾ cups

1 cup cranberries
¼ cup fresh orange juice
⅓ cup apricot jam
3 tablespoons bourbon whiskey

Combine all the ingredients in a small saucepan and bring to a boil over high heat. Reduce the heat to moderate and cook, stirring occasionally, for 2 minutes. Remove from heat and cool to room temperature. Store in a covered container in the refrigerator for up to 1 week.

Balsamic-Port Glaze

Makes about ½ cup

½ cup balsamic vinegar
½ cup port wine
2 garlic cloves, minced

Combine all the ingredients in a small saucepan and bring to a boil over high heat. Boil until reduced by half, about 5 minutes. Remove from heat and cool to room temperature. The mixture should be thick and syrupy. Store in a covered container in the refrigerator for up to 2 weeks.

Vinaigrettes

Hazelnut Vinaigrette

Makes about 1 cup

¾ cup hazelnut oil
1 garlic clove, minced
2 tablespoons seasoned rice vinegar
1 tablespoon sherry vinegar
Salt and pepper to taste

Combine the hazelnut oil and garlic in a small bowl. Using a whisk, slowly add the vinegars, whisking all the while to form a smooth emulsion. Season with salt and pepper. Store in a covered container in the refrigerator for up to 1 week.

Balsamic Vinaigrette

Makes about 1 cup

¾ cup olive oil
1 garlic clove, minced
2 tablespoons balsamic vinegar
1 tablespoon seasoned rice vinegar
Salt and pepper to taste

Combine the olive oil and garlic in a small bowl. Using a whisk, slowly add the vinegars, whisking all the while to form a smooth emulsion. Season with salt and pepper. Store in a covered container in the refrigerator for up to 1 week.

Orange Vinaigrette

Makes about 1 cup

¾ cup olive oil
1 garlic clove, minced
2 tablespoons fresh orange juice
2 tablespoons seasoned rice vinegar
Zest from 1 small orange
Salt and pepper to taste

Combine the oil and garlic in a small bowl. Using a whisk, slowly add the orange juice and vinegar, whisking all the while to form a smooth emulsion. Add the zest, salt, and pepper. Store in a covered container in the refrigerator for 1 day.

Sherry Vinaigrette

Makes about 1 cup

¾ cup olive oil
1 garlic clove, minced
2 tablespoons sherry vinegar
1 tablespoon seasoned rice vinegar
Salt and black pepper to taste

Combine the olive oil and garlic in a small bowl. Slowly add the vinegars, whisking all the while to form a smooth emulsion. Season with salt and pepper. Store in a covered container in the refrigerator for 2 or 3 days.

Spice Mixtures

Spice mixtures can be purchased at gourmet and natural food stores, but you can also make them yourself. You may purchase the spices in ground form, but I recommend buying them whole and grinding them yourself in a spice grinder, coffee mill, or a mortar. Whole spices are fresher than preground, and therefore they have more flavor.

Five-Spice Mix

This traditional Chinese blend of spices is aromatic, slightly sweet, and distinctive.

1 tablespoon ground Szechuan peppercorns (available in Asian markets)
1 tablespoon ground fennel seed
5 star anise, ground
5 whole cloves, ground
1 teaspoon ground cinnamon
1 teaspoon ground coriander

Combine all the ingredients and mix well. Store in a tightly covered jar in a cool, dry place for up to 3 months.

Four-Pepper Mix

A fruity blend of four peppers and allspice adds zip to sautéed vegetables, rice, and grains. This mixture is particularly good as a coating on steak or tenderloin.

2 tablespoons *each* whole red peppercorns, green peppercorns, black peppercorns, white peppercorns, and whole allspice

Combine all the ingredients in a spice grinder or mortar and finely grind. Store in a tightly covered jar in a cool, dry place for up to 3 months.

STUFFINGS

Stuffing is a mixture of savory ingredients to be placed in the cavity of a bird; it can also be cooked separately in the oven or on the stovetop. Stuffings usually contain some kind of starch, either in the form of finely ground bread crumbs, bread cubes, soaked bread, or fresh bread torn into small pieces. Any kind of bread can be used as long as it is compatible with the other ingredients. Rice, grains, and chestnuts are also common ingredients. Eggs are usually the binding ingredient, but a fatty meat such as sausage, bacon, or pancetta has enough fat to bind the stuffing without the use of eggs. Additional ingredients such as nuts, raisins, currants, dried fruit, tomatoes, and spices and herbs are added for flavor. Livers, giblets, and vegetables, especially greens and mushrooms, are favored by some cooks. Traditional stuffings are placed in the cavity of a bird, but some pastes and ground mixtures are meant to be placed between the skin and flesh of the bird.

Do not stuff a bird until you are ready to cook it. Fill the bird three-fourths full to allow room for the stuffing to expand. Close the openings with metal skewers and tie the legs together with cotton string. Stuffed birds usually take a little longer to cook; a good rule is 20 minutes per pound unstuffed and 25 minutes per pound stuffed. If there are any leftovers be sure to remove the stuffing from the bird before you refrigerate it. The bird and the stuffing should be kept in separate containers. Generally speaking, ½ cup of stuffing is the amount needed for 1 pound of meat. Leftover stuffing can always be baked separately and served as a side dish.

Pistachio Nut-Sausage Stuffing

Savory pork stuffing studded with pistachio nuts enhances almost any bird. This recipe uses several Indian spices, which give it an added flavor boost.

Makes about 4 cups

1 large onion, cut into small dice
3 tablespoons olive oil
3 garlic cloves, minced
1 teaspoon *each* ground coriander, fenugreek, cumin, and mace
⅓ cup dry red wine
½ pound pork sausage, removed from the casings
1 cup toasted pistachio nuts, coarsely chopped
⅓ cup finely ground dried bread crumbs

In a small, heavy saucepan, cook the onion in the olive oil over moderate heat for 15 minutes, stirring occasionally. Add the garlic and spices and cook 2 minutes over high heat. Add the red wine and boil over high heat until the wine evaporates. Remove from heat.

Crumble the sausage into a medium bowl, mixing it with your hands to make a smooth texture. Add the cooked onion mixture and mix well. Add the pistachio nuts and bread crumbs and mix well. Refrigerate until ready to use. Do not keep longer than one day.

Corn Bread and Escarole Stuffing

This rich stuffing is a favorite of book designer Tom Ingalls. It is delicious with any wild fowl as it has an assertive flavor and holds its own well with flavorful birds.

Makes 5 to 6 cups

3 cups water
⅓ cup wild rice
2 shallots, minced
3 garlic cloves, minced
2 tablespoons unsalted butter
3 tablespoons olive oil
1 head escarole, trimmed
1 tablespoon minced fresh thyme
¼ pound prosciutto, thinly sliced
½ cup ricotta cheese
½ cup grated Parmesan cheese
¼ cup pine nuts, toasted
½ cup homemade chicken stock or canned low-salt chicken broth
2 cups packaged corn bread stuffing
Salt and pepper to taste

In a large saucepan, bring the water to a boil, add the wild rice, stir, and return to a boil. Reduce the heat to moderately high and cook uncovered for 45 minutes to 1 hour, or until the rice is tender and the kernels start to burst. Drain and set aside.

In a medium saucepan, cook the shallots and garlic in the butter and olive oil over moderate heat for 5 minutes. Add the escarole and cook just until it begins to wilt. Remove the mixture from the saucepan and chop coarsely. Place in a large bowl.

Add all the remaining ingredients and the wild rice and mix well. Refrigerate until ready to use. Do not keep longer than 2 days.

STOCKS

A flavorful stock is a key ingredient for good cooking, and a good stock is the backbone of many a dish. Stocks add flavor, body, and nutrition and thus are a valuable commodity. Care should be taken when making these liquids as they can make or break a soup or sauce. By following a few simple guidelines and using fresh wholesome ingredients, you can make a stock that is good enough to be eaten alone.

The best thing to do is to save your meat and poultry bones, freezing them if necessary, until you are ready to make a big pot of stock. If you don't have any ingredients that you have saved for stock then all you need to do is make a visit to the local butcher shop. Meat bones such as beef, lamb, and pork are usually available at most good butcher shops, but if they do not have just the bones for sale, a good substitute is shank, knuckle, neck, or rib bones. Oftentimes the small amount of meat on these bones is just enough to add flavor and body to the stock. Poultry and wild fowl backs, wings, necks, feet, and carcasses are suitable for making poultry or wild fowl stock. Sometimes butcher shops have chicken bones for sale. These are generally left over from boning breasts and are great for stock. If you do not have a good supply of your own chicken bones and if the butcher only has chicken parts, take the necks, backs, and feet for your stock.

Always start with cold water, as it speeds the extraction of flavor and gelatin. Hot water delays this action because many proteins are soluble in cold water but not in hot. Boiling stock or cooking it covered makes it cloudy and bitter. When the stock is cool enough to handle, strain it through a sieve or a colander, pressing the vegetables and poultry or wild fowl bones to extract the last bit of flavor. You may remove the fat from the surface of the strained stock at this point, or you may refrigerate the stock, allow the fat to harden, and then scrape it off the surface. Be sure to save all the fat from the stock, because this flavorful ingredient can be used as a substitute for butter or oil in many recipes.

To concentrate stock or broth, strain stock then boil until reduced to half the original amount. To make a demi glace, boil in a heavy pan until thick enough to coat the back of a spoon. Use as a sauce or an addition to sauces. If time is a factor, use canned broth. There are several drawbacks to using canned stock, the first one being that they are generally very salty. Try to find unsalted or low-salt broths. Canned broth has less flavor and body than homemade stock and therefore lacks the powers of the superior product. In any case, avoid using bouillon cubes as these have a high percentage of salt and little taste.

Poultry or Wild Fowl Stock

Using the meat as well as the bones makes a rich and flavorful stock. The end product will need little if any fortification. For a more intense flavor, boil the strained stock until reduced by one half. Rabbit may be used instead of poultry or wild fowl.

Makes about 2 quarts

4 or 5 pounds poultry and/or wild fowl bones, necks, backs, and/or feet
6 quarts cold water
2 onions, coarsely chopped
5 celery stalks, coarsely chopped
2 carrots, peeled and coarsely chopped
2 bay leaves
6 parsley sprigs

Place the poultry and/or fowl bones and/or parts in a large stockpot; add the water. Bring to a boil and skim the surface. Add all the remaining ingredients and bring to a boil. Reduce the heat and simmer, uncovered, over moderate heat for about 4 to 5 hours. Cool and strain. If you are not using the stock right away you may store it in the refrigerator for up to 5 days, or freeze it for up to 3 months.

Light Poultry or Wild Fowl Stock

If you have a fairly meaty carcass left over, you can use it to make a light stock. If a stronger flavor is desired, reduce the stock by one half after straining.

Makes about 2 quarts

1 wild fowl or poultry carcass with some meat attached, cut up
2 pounds chicken necks, backs, or wings
6 quarts cold water
2 onions, coarsely chopped
5 celery stalks, coarsely chopped
2 carrots, peeled and coarsely chopped
2 bay leaves
6 parsley sprigs

Place the carcass, chicken parts, and cold water in a large stockpot. Bring to a boil. Skim the surface if necessary. Add all the remaining ingredients and bring to a boil. Reduce the heat and cook, uncovered, for 3 to 4 hours over moderate heat. Cool and strain. If you are not using the stock right away you may store it in the refrigerator for up to 5 days or freeze it for up to 3 months.

Brown Stock

You can use almost any red meat for this stock. Lamb, pork, venison, or buffalo can all be substituted for beef, but keep in mind that the stock will taste like the meat and bones that you use. Browning the bones in the oven gives the end product a richer flavor and darker color.

Makes about 2 quarts

5 pounds beef bones
6 quarts cold water
3 onions, coarsely chopped
1 head garlic, separated into unpeeled cloves
4 carrots, peeled and coarsely chopped
1 cup chopped tomato
1 cup chopped mushrooms
2 bay leaves
1 tablespoon black peppercorns

Preheat the oven to 500°. Place the bones on a flat rack in a roasting pan and roast for 45 minutes to 1 hour, or until the bones are dark brown and very aromatic. Remove from the oven.

Place the bones and cold water in a large stockpot. Bring to a boil and skim the surface. Add all the remaining ingredients and bring to a boil. Skim the surface once more. Reduce the heat and cook, uncovered, over moderate heat for 6 to 8 hours. Cool and strain. If you are not using the stock right away you may store it in the refrigerator for up to 5 days or freeze it for up to 3 months.

Appetizers, Soups, and Salads

Most of the following recipes use cooked wild or domestic fowl, so while they are fine recipes to make from scratch, they are also perfect for using leftover cooked game birds or poultry.

APPETIZERS

Wild Fowl Quesadillas

Use any fowl for these simple appetizers or snacks. Partridge is particularly good. Squab, Guinea fowl, or poussin can also be used.

Serves 3 to 6

Olive oil for cooking
6 large flour tortillas, or 12 corn tortillas
1 pound Monterey jack cheese, shredded
2 large avocados, peeled, pitted, and thinly sliced
2 cups shredded cooked wild fowl or poultry meat
Salsa Cruda, page 40

Heat a thin layer of oil (about ⅛ inch) in a large sauté pan or skillet. Place as many tortillas in the pan as will fit. Cook over low heat for 1 minute. Flip the tortillas and cover with cheese. Cook over low heat until the cheese is melted. Top with a slice of avocado and some of the meat. Fold over and serve immediately with the Salsa Cruda.

Duxelles-and-Goose-stuffed Squash

Rich and satisfying, these appetizers would also be good as a side dish to roast duck or pheasant. This stuffing can also be used for mushrooms, zucchini, or potatoes.

Serves 6

6 baby pattypan squash
1 large onion, cut into small dice
3 garlic cloves, minced
½ teaspoon *each* dried oregano, basil, sage, and thyme
3 tablespoons unsalted butter
¼ cup dry sherry
1 cup minced cooked goose meat
2 tablespoons olive oil
¾ pound mushrooms, minced
2 tablespoons mushroom soy sauce (available in Asian markets) or regular soy sauce
Salt and pepper to taste

Preheat the oven to 400°. Blanch the squash in boiling salted water for 3 minutes. Slice ½ inch off the top of each squash. Using a small spoon, carefully remove the pulp, leaving a solid shell of squash. Reserve the pulp for another use. Slice a very thin piece off the bottom of each squash so it can stand upright. Invert the squash and drain on a paper towel until ready to use.

In a large sauté pan or skillet, cook the onion, garlic, and herbs in the butter over moderate heat for 15 minutes, stirring occasionally. Add the sherry and cook over high heat for 2 minutes. Remove the mixture from the pan and place in a bowl. Add the goose meat.

In the same pan, heat the olive oil until it just starts to smoke. Add the mushrooms and cook over high heat until they are golden brown and dry, about 5 minutes. Add the mushroom soy sauce and mix well. Add to the onions and mix well. Season with salt and pepper.

Spoon the filling into the squash, forming a dome shape. Place in a greased shallow baking pan and bake for 20 minutes. Remove from the oven and serve immediately.

Chilies Filled with Smoked Chicken and Cheese

A delicious way to use up smoked chicken or turkey. You can serve this with your favorite tomato sauce in place of the Salsa Cruda. A drizzle of sour cream adds richness and flavor. Use poblano, California, long green, or hot yellow wax chilies.

Serves 6

6 large fresh green chilies, roasted
1 pound Monterey jack cheese, shredded
1 cup minced smoked chicken or turkey
2 teaspoons cumin seed
Black pepper to taste
Salsa Cruda, page 40

Preheat the oven to 400°. Make a 1-inch incision at the top of each chili; carefully peel and seed the chilies. Combine the cheese, chicken, cumin seed, and pepper in a bowl; toss to mix. Fill the chilies with the mixture, packing it in gently and taking care not to tear the chilies.

Place the filled chilies on a greased baking sheet with a rim. Bake until the cheese completely melts and the filling is hot, about 12 to 15 minutes. Spoon a pool of Salsa Cruda on individual serving plates and arrange the stuffed chilies on the salsa.

Gruyère-and-Rabbit-stuffed New Potatoes

Rich and filling, these stuffed potatoes would make a good lunch, served with a salad of bitter greens and a crisp white wine. Wild fowl or poultry may be used in place of the rabbit.

Serves 6

6 round medium new potatoes
Olive oil for roasting potatoes
3 green onions, minced
3 tablespoons unsalted butter
⅓ pound Gruyère cheese, grated
½ cup sour cream
¾ cup minced cooked rabbit
1 teaspoon ground coriander
Salt and pepper to taste

Preheat the oven to 400°. Place the potatoes in a greased baking pan and drizzle lightly with olive oil. Turn the potatoes to coat them evenly with oil. Bake until tender when pierced with a fork, about 45 minutes. Remove from the oven and let cool. When cool enough to handle, slice in half and carefully remove the pulp, taking care not to tear the skin. Set the skins aside and place the pulp in a bowl.

Cook the green onions in the butter over moderate heat for 2 minutes. Add the onions to the potato pulp. Add the cheese, sour cream, rabbit, coriander, salt, and pepper; mix well. Taste and adjust the seasoning. Stuff the mixture back into the potato skins and bake for 20 minutes at 350°. Serve the potatoes hot.

SOUPS

Cream of Chicken Soup with Three Colors

A bit lighter and more colorful than the traditional version, this cream of chicken soup can be made a day ahead, but the spinach should be added just before serving.

Serves 6 to 8

¼ cup chicken fat or olive oil
1 large onion, finely diced
2 garlic cloves, minced
3 tablespoons flour
1 teaspoon rubbed sage
1 teaspoon dried thyme
¾ cup dry white wine
6 cups homemade chicken stock or canned low-salt chicken broth
1 cup heavy cream
1 large carrot, peeled and finely diced

3 medium tomatoes, finely diced
Salt and pepper to taste
2 cups chopped cooked chicken meat
1 bunch spinach, stemmed and chopped

Melt the fat in a large, heavy pot. Cook the onion and garlic in the fat over moderate heat for 20 minutes, stirring often. Add the flour and cook for 5 minutes, stirring constantly. Add the herbs and wine and bring to a boil over high heat. Cook over high heat until the liquid has evaporated, about 5 minutes. Add the stock and bring to a boil over high heat. Boil for 15 minutes, stirring from time to time.

Over moderately low heat, add the cream, carrot, and tomatoes and simmer for 15 minutes. Taste and adjust the seasoning for salt and pepper. Just before serving, add the chicken and spinach and stir just long enough to wilt the spinach, about 10 seconds. Serve immediately.

Miso Soup with Duck and Corn

This light soup takes only minutes to prepare. You may use any leftover fowl and the appropriate stock, but duck gives the soup a particularly flavorful and rich taste. You can find miso, which is a fermented soybean product, in Asian and natural foods stores. It comes in brown, red, and white forms, but white is generally the sweetest.

Serves 4 to 6

3 tablespoons Asian (toasted) sesame oil
1 large white onion, thinly sliced
1 cup sake
6 cups duck or chicken stock or canned low-salt chicken broth
½ cup miso, preferably white
1½ cups shredded cooked duck meat
1 cup corn kernels (1 to 2 medium ears)
¼ cup chopped fresh cilantro
Black pepper to taste

Heat the oil in a large pot. Add the onion and cook over moderate heat for 5 minutes, stirring from time to time. Add the sake and cook over high heat until the liquid evaporates, 3 to 4 minutes. Add the duck stock and bring to a boil over high heat. Cook over high heat for 10 minutes. Reduce the heat to moderate; add the miso, duck, and corn and cook just until heated. Add the cilantro and black pepper and serve immediately.

Latin Turkey Soup with Pumpkin Seed Pesto

The ingredients and garnish for this hearty soup are borrowed from Latin American cuisine. The robust flavors and warm golden color of the soup are a wonderful counterpoint to the savory Pumpkin Seed Pesto.

Serves 6 to 8

2 large onions, diced
4 garlic cloves, minced
¼ cup chicken fat or olive oil
1 cup dry white wine
1½ cups chopped, peeled, and, seeded tomatoes
2 large yams, peeled and diced
1 large carrot, diced
2 quarts rich turkey or chicken stock or canned low-salt chicken broth
3 cups chopped cooked turkey meat
1 cup corn kernels (1 to 2 medium ears)
2 zucchini, halved lengthwise and sliced into ½-inch pieces
Salt and pepper to taste
Pumpkin Seed Pesto, page 43

In a large soup pot over moderate heat, cook the onions and garlic in the chicken fat for 20 minutes. Add the wine and cook until it evaporates, about 3 or 4 minutes. Add the tomatoes, yams, and carrot and cook over high heat for 2 minutes. Add the turkey stock and bring to a boil over high heat. Reduce the heat to moderate and cook the soup until the carrot and yams are tender, about 20 minutes. Add the turkey meat, corn, and zucchini and cook until the zucchini is tender, about 2 minutes. Season with salt and pepper and garnish with a dollop of Pumpkin Seed Pesto.

Cream of Tomato-Cheddar Soup with Smoked Turkey

This smooth and creamy soup is enhanced by bright green shreds of spinach. Add the spinach just before serving.

Serves 6 to 8

1 large onion, chopped
2 garlic cloves, chopped
3 tablespoons olive oil
1 tablespoon ground coriander
½ teaspoon *each* dried oregano, thyme, and sage
4 cups chopped tomatoes
6 cups light homemade chicken stock or canned low-salt chicken broth
½ cup heavy cream
½ pound sharp Cheddar cheese, shredded
2 cups chopped smoked turkey meat

Salt and pepper to taste
1 bunch spinach, stemmed, washed, and cut into thin strips

In a large soup pot, cook the onion and garlic in the olive oil over high heat for 10 minutes, stirring from time to time. Add the herbs and tomatoes and cook over high heat for 5 minutes. Add the chicken stock and bring to a boil over high heat. Reduce the heat to moderate and cook for 15 minutes. Remove from the heat and cool slightly. Transfer the mixture to a blender or food processor and puree until smooth. Strain through a fine sieve and return to the soup pot.

Bring the soup to a boil and add the cream. Reduce the heat to moderate and add the cheese, a little bit at a time, stirring all the while as it melts. When all the cheese is melted, add the turkey and heat just to warm the turkey all the way through, about 5 minutes. Season with salt and pepper and add the spinach; mix well and serve immediately.

Pheasant and Wild Rice Soup Tom Ingalls

Tom Ingalls, a friend and the designer of this and many other books, here shares his simple and delicious recipe for pheasant soup. Using a few leftovers you can have a simple but elegant soup in less than an hour. This makes a delightful first course for a late fall or winter meal.

Serves 6 to 8

1 quart water
1 cup wild rice
2 tablespoons olive oil
1 pound mushrooms, sliced medium thick
1 large onion, finely diced
3 shallots, peeled and thinly sliced
3 tablespoons duck or chicken fat or olive oil
1 cup Madeira
2 quarts homemade chicken or wild fowl stock or canned low-salt chicken broth
2 cups shredded cooked pheasant
Salt and pepper to taste

In a large saucepan, bring the water to a boil, add the rice, stir, and return to a boil. Reduce the heat to moderately high and cook uncovered for 45 minutes to 1 hour, or until the rice is tender and the kernels start to burst. Drain and set aside.

Heat the oil in a large skillet. When the oil is hot but not smoking, add the mushrooms and cook over high heat for 5 to 7 minutes, stirring all the while. When the mushrooms are golden brown and all the liquid has evaporated, transfer to a bowl and set aside until ready to use.

Over moderate heat, cook the onion and shallots in the fat for 10 to 15 minutes, stirring from time to time. Add the Madeira and bring to a boil over high heat. Reduce the heat to moderate and cook until the liquid has evaporated, about 5 minutes. Add the stock and bring to a boil over high heat. Add the rice and pheasant meat and boil for 2 or 3 minutes. Reduce the heat to moderate, add the mushrooms, and cook for 15 minutes. Season with salt and pepper.

SALADS

The following salads are not your everyday plate of greens tossed with dressing. Rather they are combinations of familiar and exotic ingredients matched with cooked fowl. Each salad can be served as a lunch entree or as a light dinner entree. Paired with a compatible soup and some interesting bread, any one of these salads would be good for a dinner with company.

When choosing greens either for the body of the salad or as a bed for other foods, look for crisp, healthy, fresh greens. An assortment of lettuces or greens usually makes a more interesting salad, but a plate of artfully arranged and carefully dressed lettuce is welcome on any table. Baby lettuce greens such as red and green leaf, mâche, red oak, butter, and romaine make a pleasant and mild salad. The bitter greens such as dandelion, endive, curly endive, escarole, and radicchio are good in combination with the slightly milder greens such as watercress, arugula (rocket), mizuna, and mustard. Red and white cabbage can add a pronounced flavor and color to some salads.

Always wash greens in cold water and be sure to dry them thoroughly. If you are not using the greens right away you can store them in a dry plastic bag in the refrigerator for up to 3 or 4 days, depending on the freshness, quality, and type of greens. Before dressing a salad, make sure the greens are very dry. Wet greens make a limp, soggy salad.

Always use good oils, vinegars, and flavoring agents when making salads. Virgin or extra-virgin olive oils have good flavor and enough body to make an excellent vinaigrette. "Fruity" olive oil refers to the flavor of the oil. Fruity oils have an assertive olive taste and are full bodied and low in acid. Green- or gold-colored extra-virgin oils are usually fruity.

Duck and Mixed Greens Salad with Pistachios

Substitute any wild fowl for the duck in this unusual salad. An interesting cheese, a bottle of wine, and some fresh bread will round out this meal.

Serves 4 to 6

Mixed greens such as dandelion, arugula, watercress, and assorted lettuces
1 small red onion, very thinly sliced
3 prunes, pitted and chopped
Orange Vinaigrette, page 45
1½ cups shredded cooked duck or any wild fowl
½ cup pistachio nuts, toasted
Freshly ground black pepper to taste

Place the greens, onion, and prunes in a large bowl. Drizzle with some of the vinaigrette and toss. Dress the duck with some of the vinaigrette. Place the greens on a large platter or individual plates. Top with the duck and garnish with the pistachio nuts. Dust with black pepper.

Thai-Style Duck Salad with Noodles

This slightly Americanized version of a Thai salad is light and spicy. Don't be scared off by the long list of ingredients. The assembly is fast and easy.

Serves 4 to 6

Dressing
½ cup olive oil
¼ cup fish sauce (available in Asian markets)
Juice of 2 limes
1 teaspoon sugar
3 garlic cloves, minced
1 serrano chili, minced
Ground black pepper to taste

Salad
⅓ pound cellophane noodles
2 cups shredded cooked free-range chicken or duck
1 small cucumber, peeled, seeded, and cut into ¼-inch slices
1 cup bean sprouts
1 small red onion, thinly sliced
⅔ cup peanuts, toasted and chopped
Cilantro sprigs, for garnish

Combine the dressing ingredients in a small bowl; mix well and set aside at room temperature. Bring a large pot of water to a boil. In a bowl, soak the noodles in cold water to cover for 2 to 3 minutes. Drain and cook in the boiling water for 2 to 3 minutes, or until tender. Drain and dry thoroughly.

Dress the noodles with some of the dressing and place on a large platter. Dress the chicken with some of the dressing. Arrange the chicken and vegetables on top of the noodles. Garnish with the peanuts and cilantro and serve at room temperature. Pass the remaining dressing.

Composed Summer Vegetable Salad with Goose

Any fowl will work in this elegant salad, but goose or duck is particularly good as they are moist and very flavorful. This makes a wonderful summer lunch entree or a generous first course for dinner.

Serves 4

1 boneless goose breast (about 1 pound)
¼ pound fettuccine
1 small red bell pepper, finely diced
1 cup corn kernels (1 to 2 medium ears)
6 asparagus, trimmed and sliced ½ inch thick on the diagonal
Balsamic Vinaigrette, page 45
⅓ cup toasted pecans, chopped
Mixed greens such as arugula, watercress, curly endive, and assorted lettuces

In a sauté pan or skillet over moderate heat, fry the goose breast, turning it to cook evenly until skin is brown and meat is just pink in the center, about 15 minutes. Allow it to rest for 20 minutes before slicing. Slice on the diagonal and set aside. Cook the pasta until it is al dente. Drain well and place in a bowl with the pepper and corn. Blanch the asparagus for 30 seconds and add to the pasta and vegetables. Dress lightly with Balsamic Vinaigrette and toss gently. Just before serving, garnish the pasta with the chopped pecans. Toss the greens with a little vinaigrette. Arrange the greens, pasta salad, and sliced goose breast on a large platter or on individual plates. Serve at room temperature.

Chicken Salad with Cashews and Olives

Here is a chicken salad that combines crunchy, salty, and sweet all in one bowl. Add the cashews just before serving to prevent them from becoming soggy. Pheasant can be used in place of chicken for this salad.

Serves 4 to 6

1 medium onion, finely diced
¼ cup seasoned rice vinegar
1 cup mayonnaise
3 tablespoons red wine vinegar
1 tablespoon dry mustard
1 teaspoon dried basil
½ teaspoon cayenne pepper
3 cups diced cooked free-range chicken
1 cup diced celery
¾ cup green olives, pitted and coarsely chopped
1 cup cashews, toasted
Salt and pepper to taste
1 small bunch escarole, trimmed and torn into medium pieces

In a small bowl, soak the onion in the vinegar for 30 minutes. Drain and discard the vinegar. Place the onions in a large bowl.

In a small bowl, combine the mayonnaise, red wine vinegar, mustard, basil, and cayenne; mix well. Add the chicken, celery, and olives to the onions and combine with the mayonnaise mixture. Add half the cashews and season with salt and pepper.

Place the greens on a large platter and arrange the chicken mixture on top. Garnish with the remaining cashews. Serve at room temperature.

GAME
AND
WINE
MENUS

Duck is flavorful, rich, and pleasantly fatty. Sometimes cooks make the mistake of failing to release the excess fat or of cooking the duck too long so that it dries out. If you follow the directions closely you won't be disappointed. There are a number of wild and domestic ducks from which to choose, but this recipe uses the Pekin duck most commonly found in Asian markets. You can find all of the other ingredients in any Asian market.

Serves 4

Green Onion Cakes with Fire-Prune Dipping Sauce

The sauce improves the second day, after the flavors have had time to blend; the batter can be made a day ahead as well. The delicate crepelike pancakes should be cooked just before serving.

1 cup unbleached all-purpose flour
1 cup homemade chicken stock or low-salt canned chicken broth
3 tablespoons Asian (toasted) sesame oil
3 tablespoons rice vinegar
4 eggs, lightly beaten
3 garlic cloves, thinly sliced
1 teaspoon ground black pepper
6 green onions, minced
Vegetable oil for cooking
Fire-Prune Dipping Sauce, page 39
Cilantro sprigs for garnish

Place the flour in a medium bowl. Combine the chicken stock, sesame oil, vinegar, and eggs. Slowly add this mixture to the flour, stirring constantly to form a smooth paste. Add the garlic, pepper, and green onions; mix well. Cover and refrigerate for at least 2 hours, or until the batter coats the back of a spoon and is the consistency of heavy cream.

Heat a thin layer of oil in a 6-inch nonstick sauté pan or skillet. When the oil is hot but not smoking, spoon 3 to 4 tablespoons of the batter into the pan, swirling the batter to the edges of the pan, as if you were making crepes or a thin omelette. Cook over moderate heat for about 1 minute. When the edges begin to turn golden brown, flip the pancake and cook the second side until golden brown. Cook the remaining batter in this fashion, keeping the pancakes warm in a low oven.

Fold the pancakes in quarters and serve with the sauce. Garnish the plate with sprigs of cilantro.

Five-Spice Roast Duck

A Chinese-inspired spice mix gives this dish a subtle but fragrant flavor. Simple and easy to prepare, the duck takes care of itself in the oven while you prepare the rest of the meal.

One 5- to 5½-pound duck
1 orange, halved
1 onion, halved
2½ tablespoons Five-Spice Mix, page 45

Preheat the oven to 500°. Pat the duck dry with paper towels. Place the orange and onion in the cavity. Using a fork, prick the duck all over, just through the skin to the meat. Rub the duck all over with the spice mix and place on a flat rack in a roasting pan.

Place the duck in the oven for 10 minutes, then reduce the heat to 400° and roast for about 15 to 20 minutes per pound. Prick the skin every 20 minutes to release the fat. When the bird is golden brown and the juices run clear when the underside is pricked with a fork, remove the bird from the oven and allow it to rest for 7 to 10 minutes before carving.

Braised Sesame Eggplant with Peppers

This dark and savory dish makes a fine match with the bright stir-fried vegetables. It tastes even better if made the day before and reheated just before serving.

1 large onion, cut in wedges
3 tablespoons olive oil
¼ cup Asian (toasted) sesame oil
5 garlic cloves, minced
1 jalapeño chili, cored, seeded, and sliced thin
2 Japanese eggplants, halved lengthwise and cut into ½-inch diagonal slices, or 1 globe eggplant, cut into ½-inch dice
1 cup dry white wine or sake
3 tablespoons soy sauce
3 tablespoons Chinese black rice vinegar
½ teaspoon ground black pepper
1 large red bell pepper, cut into 1-by-½-inch slices
¼ cup toasted sesame seeds
¼ cup chopped fresh cilantro

Cook the onion in the olive oil and sesame oil over high heat for 5 minutes, stirring constantly. Add the garlic, jalapeño, and eggplants and cook over high heat for 3 minutes, stirring constantly. Add the wine, soy sauce, vinegar, and black pepper, reduce the heat to moderate, and cook for 15 minutes. Add the bell pepper and cook until tender, about 10 minutes, stirring occasionally. Garnish with the sesame seeds and cilantro.

Stir-Fried Chinese Vegetables
Page 120

FIVE-SPICE ROAST DUCK

Green Onion Cakes with Fire-
Prune Dipping Sauce
Five-Spice Roast Duck
Braised Sesame Eggplant with
Peppers
Stir-fried Chinese Vegetables

Beaujolais-Villages or Merlot

Boned duck breasts make this meal simple and elegant at the same time. Fan out the sliced meat and drizzle with the sauce for an attractive presentation. Colorful glazed vegetables are a tasty companion to mashed turnips. You may substitute a potato for one of the turnips if a milder flavor is desired.

Serves 4

Broiled Duck Breast with Balsamic-Raspberry Sauce

Tender, rosy duck meat is delightful with a slightly tart raspberry sauce.

2 whole Muscovy, Mallard, or Moulard duck breasts, boned
Balsamic-Raspberry Sauce, page 39

Preheat the broiler. Prick the skin of the duck breasts with a fork. Cook under the broiler, skin side up, until golden brown, about 5 minutes. Turn the breasts and cook the other side for 3 to 5 minutes. Remove from the oven and let rest for 5 minutes.

Slice the duck breast on the diagonal into ¼-inch-thick slices and serve on a pool of the sauce. Drizzle a little sauce over the top of the sliced duck and serve immediately.

Glazed Green Beans and Carrots

A winning duo. Carrots and beans made shiny by the addition of a bit of sugar and butter are good with almost any classic game dish.

1 bunch baby carrots (about 8), peeled and halved lengthwise
½ pound green beans, trimmed
1 tablespoon butter
½ cup homemade chicken or duck stock or canned low-salt chicken
  broth
1 teaspoon sugar
Salt and pepper to taste

Blanch the carrots and beans in boiling salted water to cover for 1 minute. Drain and dry on paper towels.

Place the butter and stock in a sauté pan or skillet. Place over high heat until the butter melts. Add the carrots and beans and cook for 2 to 3 minutes. When the liquid has almost evaporated, add the sugar and cook over high heat for 1 more minute. Season with salt and pepper and serve immediately.

Buttered Mashed Turnips

Let's face it, root vegetables taste good with a lot of butter. You can cut down on the amount of butter in this recipe, but the turnips won't be as delicious.

2 large turnips (about 1⅓ pounds), peeled and quartered
4 tablespoons unsalted butter
1 teaspoon sugar
Pinch nutmeg
¼ cup minced fresh parsley
Salt and pepper to taste

Cook the turnips in boiling salted water to cover until very tender, 25 to 30 minutes. Drain and mash with a fork to form a slightly lumpy mixture. Add the butter, sugar, and nutmeg. Return to a small sauté pan or skillet and cook for 5 minutes over moderate heat. Add the parsley, salt, and pepper and serve immediately.

BROILED DUCK BREAST WITH BALSAMIC-RASPBERRY SAUCE

Broiled Duck Breast with
Balsamic-Raspberry Sauce
Glazed Green Beans and Carrots
Buttered Mashed Turnips

St. Julien

CORIANDER-THYME ROAST DUCK BREAST

Mixed Greens with Hazelnut
Vinaigrette
Coriander-Thyme Roast Duck
Breast
Potato-Leek Gratin
Apple, Beet, and Carrot Sauté

Gigondas

Succulent duck breast teamed with a rich, creamy potato gratin makes a memorable meal for family or friends. Roasting the duck ensures a juicy and perfectly cooked product with little fuss.

Serves 4 to 6

Mixed Greens with Hazelnut Vinaigrette

6 cups assorted greens such as arugula, mustard, mizuna, dandelion,
    frisée, mâche, radicchio, and assorted lettuces
Hazelnut Vinaigrette, page 45
½ cup hazelnuts, skinned and chopped

Wash and thoroughly dry the greens. Place in a large bowl and drizzle with the vinaigrette. Toss and arrange on individual plates or one large platter. Garnish with hazelnuts.

Coriander-Thyme Roast Duck Breast

1 tablespoon ground coriander
3 tablespoons minced fresh thyme, or 2 teaspoons dried thyme
3 garlic cloves, minced
2 whole Mallard or Barbarie duck breasts, boned (about 4 pounds total)

Preheat the oven to 400°. In a small bowl, combine the coriander, thyme, and garlic to form a paste. Rub the breasts all over with the paste and prick the skin with a fork. Place the breasts on a flat rack in a roasting pan.

Roast for about 15 minutes or until the meat is pink in the middle. Let the duck rest for 5 minutes before slicing. Cut into thin slices and serve immediately.

Potato-Leek Gratin

This easy potato dish can be cooked on top of the stove and served hot or at room temperature.

2 large leeks, halved lengthwise and sliced ½ inch thick
4 tablespoons unsalted butter
2 garlic cloves, minced
2 cups heavy cream
2 teaspoons dried basil
½ teaspoon salt
1 teaspoon ground black pepper
2 tablespoons olive oil
2½ pounds new white potatoes, peeled and sliced ¼ inch thick

In a 12-inch nonstick sauté pan or skillet, cook the leeks in 2 tablespoons of the butter over high heat for 10 minutes. Combine the cooked leeks, garlic, cream, basil, salt, and pepper in a bowl; mix well.

Using the same pan, melt the remaining 2 tablespoons butter and the oil over moderate heat. When the butter is melted, arrange the potatoes in a circular fashion, slightly overlapping the slices. When all the potatoes have been used, return the pan to high heat and cook for 3 to 4 minutes, pressing down on the potatoes with your hands. Distribute the leek-cream mixture evenly over the top and cook over high heat for 2 minutes. Reduce the heat to moderate and cook until the potatoes are tender, the cream has thickened, and the mixture is set, about 40 to 45 minutes. Remove from the heat and let stand for 15 minutes before slicing into wedges.

Apple, Beet, and Carrot Sauté

Fall flavors and colors make this appetizing vegetable dish a pleasure for all the senses. Golden beets would make a beautiful addition to the combination.

3 small red beets
6 baby carrots, peeled and halved lengthwise
2 tablespoons unsalted butter
2 tart green apples, thinly sliced
Juice of 1 lemon
Salt and pepper to taste

Cook the beets in boiling salted water to cover until they are tender, 20 to 25 minutes. When cool enough to handle, peel and quarter. Cook the carrots in boiling salted water until tender, 5 to 7 minutes. Drain and dry on paper towels.

Melt the butter in a saucepan. Add the carrots and apples and cook over low heat until heated all the way through, about 5 minutes. Heat the beets with the lemon juice in a separate pan. Season the beets, carrots, and apples with salt and pepper. Place the carrots and apples on the serving platter and garnish with the beets.

This menu might sound light because it consists of only a soup, salad, and bread sticks, but it actually makes a substantial meal. Any smoked fowl can be used, but smoked duck is especially delicious and truly complements the cabbage salad ingredients.

Serves 6

Warm Red Cabbage Salad with Smoked Duck

Warm red cabbage is a traditional dish found throughout eastern and southern Europe. It can be prepared with an assortment of ingredients depending on the region, the chef, and the time of year. This salad version is colorful and complex in texture and flavor. If all the ingredients will not fit in your pan at one time, split them in half and make the salad in two batches. Be sure the oil is smoking hot before adding the ingredients.

⅓ cup fruity olive oil
1 medium red onion, thinly sliced
3 garlic cloves, minced
4 cups finely shredded red cabbage
1 red bell pepper, cut into julienne
1 teaspoon dried red pepper flakes
3 tablespoons balsamic vinegar
1½ cups shredded fresh spinach
2½ cups shredded smoked duck meat
¾ cup pistachio nuts, toasted
Salt and pepper to taste

Heat the oil in a very large sauté pan or skillet over high heat until it is smoking. Add the onion, garlic, red cabbage, bell pepper, and red pepper flakes and cook for 2 minutes, stirring constantly. Add the vinegar, spinach, and duck; mix well and cook 1 minute. Arrange on a large platter and garnish with the pistachio nuts. Season and serve immediately.

Thyme and Rosemary Bread Sticks

Served fresh from the oven, these slightly salty bread sticks are a wonderful snack any time of day with a green salad or just a glass of wine. These are best baked on a pizza stone, but if you don't have one you can use a baking sheet instead.

1½ cups unbleached bread flour
½ teaspoon salt
1¼ teaspoons active dry yeast
½ cup warm (105° to 115°) water
3 tablespoons olive oil
½ cup fruity olive oil
4 garlic cloves, minced
2 tablespoons minced fresh rosemary
2 tablespoons minced fresh thyme
Kosher salt for sprinkling

Preheat the oven to 500°. Place the flour and salt in a large mixing bowl. In a small bowl, dissolve the yeast in the water and stir to form a paste. Add the 3 tablespoons olive oil to the yeast mixture and mix well. Add the yeast mixture to the flour and salt and stir to form a dough. Turn out on a lightly floured surface and knead the dough for 3 to 4 minutes, or until elastic and smooth. Place in a greased bowl, turn to coat all sides, and cover with a damp cloth. Let rise in a warm place until doubled in size, about 1 hour. Punch down the dough and turn it out on a lightly floured surface. Knead the dough for 2 minutes. Cover with a cloth and let rest for 15 to 20 minutes. Meanwhile, preheat a pizza stone in the oven for 15 minutes if you wish.

   In a small bowl, combine the fruity olive oil and the garlic. Roll the dough out to a thickness of ¼ inch. Brush the dough with the garlic oil, sprinkle with rosemary and thyme, and cut into long strips 1 inch wide. Fold each strip in half the long way so that the oiled surfaces come together. Twist the strips to make thick ribbons. Place the ribbons on the preheated pizza stone or a baking sheet, brush generously with more garlic oil, and sprinkle with salt. Bake until golden brown, about 10 to 12 minutes. Remove from the oven and brush with the garlic oil. Serve warm or at room temperature.

Winter Squash Soup with Orange Crème Fraîche
Page 120

WARM RED CABBAGE SALAD WITH SMOKED DUCK

Winter Squash Soup with Orange
Crème Fraîche
*Warm Red Cabbage Salad with
Smoked Duck*
*Thyme and Rosemary
Bread Sticks*

Sauvignon Blanc or Alsatian
Gewürztraminer

ROAST FOUR-PEPPER PHEASANT

Mild and Bitter Greens with
Asiago Croutons and Balsamic
Vinaigrette
Roast Four-Pepper Pheasant
Maple-braised Brussels Sprouts
Pecan Wild Rice

Merlot

In my opinion, pheasant is one of the most rewarding birds available. Sweet, tender meat and the perfect amount of fat for flavor and moisture make pheasant good for grilling, roasting, or for stews. Both farm-raised and wild pheasant are quite mild compared to most wild fowl, but still delicious and flavorful. One medium pheasant is enough for 2 people.

Serves 4

Mild and Bitter Greens with Asiago Croutons and Balsamic Vinaigrette

You may serve the cheese croutons hot or at room temperature. If you cannot find Asiago, a hard grating cheese, substitute Parmesan.

1 small baguette, sliced ¼ inch thick on the diagonal
¼ cup olive oil
¼ pound Asiago cheese, grated
4 cups assorted mild and bitter greens such as dandelion, arugula, escarole, endive, watercress, butter lettuce, mâche, or red leaf lettuce
Balsamic Vinaigrette, page 45

Preheat the oven to 350°. Brush the bread slices with the olive oil. Arrange on a baking sheet and bake for 7 to 10 minutes, or until the croutons are barely golden. Remove from the oven and leave on the pan. When cool, top with grated cheese. Return to the oven and heat just until the cheese melts and is bubbly, about 3 minutes. Remove from the oven and set aside until ready to use.

Place the greens in a large mixing bowl and drizzle with the vinaigrette. Toss and serve immediately, with the croutons on the side of the salad.

Roast Four-Pepper Pheasant

A piquant and aromatic pepper mix adds a subtle flavor to this terrific roast pheasant.

2 medium pheasants (about 3 ½ pounds each)
3 tablespoons Five-Pepper Mix, page 45
2 oranges, halved
8 to 10 thick slices fatty bacon

Preheat the oven to 475°. Rub the birds inside and out with the Five-Pepper Mix. Place 2 orange halves inside the cavity of each pheasant. Cover the breast and legs of each bird with the bacon.

Place the birds on a flat rack in a roasting pan and cook for 10 minutes. Reduce the heat to 375° and roast until the juices run clear when the underside is pierced with a fork, about 50 to 55 minutes.

Allow the pheasants to rest for 5 minutes before carving. Cut into serving portions and serve immediately with some of the juices from the pan.

Maple-braised Brussels Sprouts

The assertive taste of Brussels sprouts is complemented by the sweetness of the maple syrup.

1 pound Brussels sprouts, trimmed and halved
2 tablespoons chicken fat or unsalted butter
1 cup homemade chicken stock or canned low-salt chicken broth
2 tablespoons pure maple syrup
Salt and pepper to taste

Cook the Brussels sprouts in the chicken fat over moderate heat for 2 minutes. Add the chicken stock and bring to a boil. Reduce the heat to moderate, cover, and cook until almost tender, about 15 minutes. Uncover and bring to a boil. When almost all the liquid has evaporated, add the maple syrup, salt, and pepper; mix well.

Pecan Wild Rice

The naturally nutty flavor of wild rice is enhanced by the addition of toasted pecans. For a lighter rice dish, substitute long-grain white rice for half of the wild rice. Cook the white rice separately and add to the cooked wild rice, fluffing with a fork just before serving.

1 medium onion, cut into small dice
3 garlic cloves, minced
3 tablespoons unsalted butter
1 cup wild rice, washed
5 cups water
1 cup pecans, toasted and chopped
Salt and pepper to taste

Cook the onion and garlic in the butter over moderate heat for 10 minutes, stirring occasionally. Add the rice and cook 1 minute. Add the water and bring to a boil. Reduce the heat to moderate and cook for 45 minutes to 1 hour, or until the rice kernels have burst. The rice should be slightly chewy, but tender. Drain excess water from the rice. Add the pecans, salt, and pepper and toss with a fork.

This menu uses baby pheasant, which is usually the perfect size for 1 hungry person. An adult pheasant may be used instead, but individual servings make an elegant and special presentation.

Serves 4

Wild Mushroom Soup with Herb Croutons

Intense and woodsy, this soup is simple in preparation but complex in taste. Use a large pan and make sure the oil is very hot before you add the mushrooms. The most common mistakes made when cooking mushrooms are using too small a pan and not using enough heat, a combination that stews the fungi instead of searing them.

2 ounces dried porcini mushrooms
1 large onion, finely diced
3 garlic cloves, minced
7 tablespoons olive oil
2 tablespoons unsalted butter
½ cup dry Marsala wine
2 quarts homemade beef stock or canned low-salt beef broth
⅓ pound fresh white cultivated mushrooms, sliced ½ inch thick
⅓ pound fresh porcini mushrooms, sliced ½ inch thick
¼ pound fresh chanterelle mushrooms
Salt and pepper to taste
½ baguette, sliced into ¼-inch-thick rounds
1 cup olive oil
1 teaspoon *each* dried thyme, oregano, sage, and basil

Preheat the oven to 400°. Soak the dried mushrooms in warm water for 10 minutes. Drain, discarding the water. With your hands, rub the mushrooms under running water to remove any grit or sand. Cut into ½-inch-thick slices and set aside.

In a saucepan, cook the onion and garlic in 3 table-spoons of the olive oil and the butter over moderate heat for 10 minutes. Add the Marsala wine and boil over high heat until the liquid evaporates, about 3 minutes. Add the stock and dried mushrooms and boil for 10 minutes. Reduce heat to moderate and cook for 20 minutes.

Wash the fresh mushrooms and dry them on paper towels. Heat the remaining 4 tablespoons of oil in a large sauté pan or skillet over high heat. When the oil is hot and just begins to smoke, add the white and porcini mushrooms and cook, stirring often, until golden brown, about 5 to 10 minutes. Add the chanterelles and cook 2 minutes. Add the cooked mushrooms to the beef stock and mix well. Cook over moderate heat for 15 minutes, taste, and season with salt and pepper.

Brush both sides of the sliced baguette generously with olive oil. Place on a baking sheet and bake until golden brown, about 7 to 10 minutes. Remove from the oven and brush again with olive oil. Combine the herbs and sprinkle on the croutons. Garnish each serving of soup with 1 or 2 croutons.

Roast Pheasant with Sun-dried Tomatoes

The robust flavors of sun-dried tomatoes and smoky bacon turn a simple roast pheasant into a memorable dish.

1 cup sun-dried tomatoes, minced
1 cup minced bacon (about ⅓ pound)
4 baby pheasants, about 1¼ pounds each
Ground black pepper to taste

Preheat the oven to 450°. Combine the sun-dried tomatoes and bacon in a bowl; mix well. With your hands, separate the skin from the meat along the breast and legs of the bird so that you can slide the mixture between the skin and the meat of the pheasants. Truss, dust with black pepper, and place on a flat rack in a greased roasting pan.

Roast for 5 minutes, breast side up. Gently turn the pheasants over and roast for 10 to 15 minutes, breast side down. Remove from the oven and serve immediately. You may halve the birds before serving, but a whole bird looks attractive on an individual plate.

Gorgonzola Polenta

Thick, rich, and golden, this soft polenta dish is pure simplicity. To reheat leftover polenta, place it in the top pan of a double boiler, add a little water, then heat until the polenta is soft again.

4 cups water
2 tablespoons unsalted butter
½ teaspoon *each* salt and ground black pepper
1½ cups polenta
¼ pound Asiago cheese, grated
¼ pound Gorgonzola cheese, crumbled
½ teaspoon dried red pepper flakes
¼ cup minced fresh parsley

Place the water, butter, salt, and pepper in a heavy pot. Bring to a boil and slowly add the polenta, whisking all the while. When the water returns to a boil, reduce the heat to moderate and cook for 15 to 20 minutes, stirring frequently, until the polenta is pale yellow and creamy. Add the cheeses and red pepper flakes; stir constantly as the cheese melts. Taste and adjust the seasoning. Garnish with parsley and serve in shallow bowls.

Sautéed Zucchini
Page 121

ROAST PHEASANT
WITH SUN-DRIED TOMATOES

*Wild Mushroom Soup with Herb
Croutons
Roast Pheasant with Sun-dried
Tomatoes
Gorgonzola Polenta
Sautéed Zucchini*

Chardonnay

BRAISED PHEASANT WITH SOUR CREAM AND GRAPES

Carrot and Parsnip Soup
with Orange
Braised Pheasant with Sour Cream
and Grapes
Scallion and Mushroom Wild Rice

Chablis or Alsatian Riesling

This recipe uses a large adult pheasant, which has a more pronounced flavor and a chewy texture. Slow cooking with plenty of moisture guarantees a juicy and satisfying dish. Simple and rich, this meal is good for company, as there is very little last-minute preparation involved. A large free-range chicken or a capon is a good substitute for the pheasant in this menu.

Serves 4

Braised Pheasant with Sour Cream and Grapes

The smoky flavor of bacon is perfect with juicy sweet grapes in this simple fall or winter dish.

¾ pound bacon
One 4- to 4½-pound pheasant, cut into serving pieces
6 shallots, sliced
3 tablespoons minced fresh thyme, or 1 tablespoon dried thyme
5 to 7 cups homemade chicken stock or canned low-salt chicken broth
1¼ cups sour cream
1½ cups halved seedless green grapes
Salt and pepper to taste

In a large sauté pan or skillet over high heat, cook the bacon until crisp. Remove with a slotted spoon and drain on paper towels. When cool, chop coarsely. Discard all but ⅓ cup of the fat.

Heat the reserved bacon fat over high heat in the same pan. Cook the pheasant in the fat in batches, removing each piece to a large kettle as it turns golden brown. When all the pheasant has been browned and placed in the kettle, add the shallots, thyme, and 5 cups of the chicken stock. Bring to a boil, reduce heat to moderate, and cook, covered, for 1 hour. Remove the cover and cook until tender, about 45 to 50 minutes. Remove the pheasant from the kettle with a slotted spoon, reserving the liquid. When cool enough to handle, remove the meat from the bones and set aside.

Meanwhile, over high heat, reduce the cooking liquid to about 1¾ cups. If there is not that much cooking liquid left, add stock until it measures 2½ cups, then reduce over high heat to 1¾ cups. Reduce the heat to moderate and add the sour cream, little by little, stirring all the while to make a smooth sauce. Add the grapes and pheasant and mix well. Add the cooked bacon. Taste and adjust the seasoning with salt and pepper. Serve on top of or alongside the rice.

Scallion and Mushroom Wild Rice

A delicate blend of wild and white rices that makes a good side dish to accompany almost any fowl. The rices must be prepared separately because they have different cooking times.

3 cups water
¾ cup long-grain white rice
⅓ cup wild rice
3 cups water
¾ pound white cultivated mushrooms, chopped
3 tablespoons chicken fat or olive oil
6 green onions (scallions), including the green tops, chopped
3 tablespoons unsalted butter
Salt and pepper to taste

Bring 3 cups of lightly salted water to a boil in a medium saucepan. Add the white rice and cook over high heat until tender, about 10 to 15 minutes. Drain and set aside until ready to use. Rinse the wild rice under cold running water. Bring 3 cups of water to a boil in a medium saucepan. Add the rice and cook over high heat until tender, about 40 to 45 minutes. Drain and set aside.

In a large skillet, cook the mushrooms in the chicken fat over high heat for 5 to 7 minutes, stirring frequently. Add the green onions and cook for 2 minutes. Add the cooked rices and butter and heat thoroughly, using a fork to toss the rice with the other ingredients. Season with salt and pepper and serve immediately.

Carrot and Parsnip Soup with Orange
Page 121

Goose is known for its high fat content and dark, tender meat. The two in combination make this one of the more succulent and flavorful fowls. Although the birds usually weigh in at 12 to 14 pounds each, the amount of meat may not be as much as you think. Allow about 2 pounds per person when purchasing your goose.

Serves 6

Orange and Fennel Salad with Parmesan

At once sweet, tart, nutty, and bitter, this salad brings many sensations to the palate.

1 small red onion, sliced paper thin
3 tablespoons seasoned rice vinegar
2 large fennel bulbs, thinly sliced
2 large oranges, peeled and sectioned
Orange Vinaigrette, page 45
1 large bunch watercress, stemmed
2 ounces Parmigiano Reggiano cheese
Coarsely ground black pepper

In a small bowl, soak the onion in the vinegar for 30 minutes. Drain and discard vinegar. Dry the onions on paper towels and set aside.

Place the fennel, orange sections, and onions in a medium bowl. Dress with some of the vinaigrette. Place the watercress on a platter or individual plates. Top with the vegetables and fruit. Using a vegetable peeler, shave the Parmesan onto the salads, using 3 or 4 shavings per salad. Dust with black pepper and serve at room temperature.

Roast Goose with Red Pepper Sauce

Goose is a great choice for lovers of dark meat. Like duck, it has lots of fat, so be sure to remove the fat around the cavity of the bird before roasting. Pricking the skin all over allows the fat to drip out as it cooks.

One 11- to 13-pound goose
2 onions, halved
2 oranges, halved
Ground black pepper for dusting
Red Pepper Sauce, page 40

Preheat the oven to 450°. Remove the deposits of fat inside the cavity of the bird. Prick the skin all over with a fork. Place the onions and oranges in the cavity. Place the goose, breast side up, on a V-shaped rack in a greased roasting pan and dust with black pepper. Roast for 1 hour, pricking the skin but not the flesh with a fork every 30 minutes or so. Reduce the oven temperature to 375° and roast until the juices run clear when the underside is pierced with a fork, about 15 to 20 minutes per pound. Remove the goose from the oven and let rest for 10 minutes before carving.

Serve with a drizzle of Red Pepper Sauce or in a pool of the sauce.

Almond Yam Cakes

These sweet, nutty cakes would be great for breakfast topped with a drizzle of maple syrup. As is, they are a unique accompaniment to the goose and green beans.

6 large yams, peeled and quartered
1 large onion, finely diced
1 tablespoon ground coriander
¼ teaspoon *each* ground mace, ground cinnamon, ground nutmeg, and cayenne
4 tablespoons unsalted butter
Salt and pepper to taste
All-purpose flour for coating cakes
2 eggs, lightly beaten
2½ cups ground almonds
Olive oil for cooking

Cook the yams in salted boiling water to cover until tender, but not mushy, about 30 to 40 minutes. Drain well and place in a bowl. Using a fork, mash the yams to form a fairly smooth paste.

Cook the onion and spices in butter over moderate heat for 20 to 25 minutes, or until the onion is golden brown, stirring frequently. Add to the yams and mix well. Season with salt and pepper. Cover and refrigerate for 2 hours or overnight.

Using about 2½ teaspoons per cake, form the yam mixture into small patties. Coat each cake with some flour, then dip into the eggs and coat thoroughly. Dip into the almonds, coating evenly. Refrigerate for at least 1 hour.

In a large nonstick sauté pan or skillet, heat about ½ inch oil over moderate heat. When the oil is hot but not smoking, add the cakes in batches, taking care not to crowd the pan. Cook, turning once, until both sides are golden brown. Drain on paper towels or keep warm in a low oven.

Sautéed Green Beans
Page 121

ROAST GOOSE WITH RED PEPPER SAUCE

Orange and Fennel Salad with
Parmesan
Roast Goose with Red Pepper
Sauce
Sautéed Green Beans
Almond Yam Cakes

Barolo or Châteauneuf-du-Pape

This Italian-inspired meal has a contemporary feeling. You may use any combination of smoked and fresh fowl to fill the ravioli, but the pairing of goose and duck makes a delicate and unforgettable filling. Purchase sheets of fresh pasta or make your own from a favorite recipe. If neither is available, use manicotti tubes or large pasta shells for filling.

Serves 6

Smoked Duck and Goose Ravioli with Snow Pea and Red Pepper Ragout

Don't let the amount of butter in the ragout scare you off! The silky texture and rich taste of the sauce comes from using butter, and plenty of it. Divided among 6 people it really isn't so much, and it's fun to indulge yourself once in a while. Make the ragout just before cooking the pasta so that the ravioli can be combined with the sauce as soon as they are drained.

Makes about 50 to 55 ravioli

Ravioli
1 medium onion, finely diced
¼ cup olive oil
4 garlic cloves, minced
½ teaspoon *each* ground mace, dried oregano, dried basil, and dried thyme
1 cup *each* minced smoked duck and minced smoked goose meat
1 pound whole-milk ricotta cheese
½ cup pine nuts, toasted and coarsely chopped
1 cup freshly grated Parmesan cheese
Salt and pepper to taste
2 pounds thin egg pasta sheets

Snow Pea and Red Pepper Ragout, following

To make the ravioli: Cook the onion in the olive oil over moderate heat for 5 minutes, stirring often. Add the garlic, spice, and herbs and cook over low heat 5 minutes. Remove from the heat, transfer to a large bowl, and let cool. Add the smoked duck, goose, ricotta cheese, pine nuts, and Parmesan cheese; mix well. Scoop up 1 tablespoon of the mixture and form it into a small ball. Cook the filling in a little simmering water. Taste and adjust for salt and pepper.

On a flat surface lay out 1 sheet of pasta. Lightly spray or brush with some water (this will help the sheets adhere to each other when you top one piece with another and prevent the pasta from drying out). Cut the sheet into 2½-inch-wide strips. Top each strip with rounded tea-

spoonfuls of filling in a straight line, leaving a space of about 1½ inches between each mound.

Cut a second sheet of pasta into 2½-inch-wide strips. Place the second strip of pasta over the first strip and gently press the strips together, force out any air, and secure the dough around the filling. With a ravioli cutter, cut into square ravioli. Make sure the pasta is closed tight around the edges or else the filling will come out during cooking. Place the filled ravioli on a flour-dusted baking sheet and cover with plastic wrap until ready to use. Make all the ravioli in this fashion and refrigerate for at least 1 hour or up to 1 day before cooking.

To cook the ravioli: Bring a large pot of salted water to a rapid boil. Gently drop the ravioli into the water and stir with a wooden spoon until the water returns to a slow boil. If the water is boiling too fiercely the ravioli will burst, but the water must be moving in order to cook the ravioli properly and to prevent them from sticking to one another. Cook until tender, 5 to 7 minutes, depending on the thickness of the pasta. With a wire mesh utensil or slotted spoon, carefully lift the ravioli from the water, draining well. Place the ravioli in individual serving bowls and top with the ragout. Serve immediately.

Snow Pea and Red Pepper Ragout
2 large onions, sliced
2 garlic cloves, thinly sliced
3 tablespoons olive oil
¾ cup dry white wine
2½ cups rich homemade chicken or duck stock or canned low-salt chicken broth
2 medium red bell peppers, cored, seeded, and cut into julienne
½ pound snow peas, trimmed and halved lengthwise
7 tablespoons unsalted butter
Salt and pepper to taste

In a sauté pan or skillet, cook the onions and garlic in the olive oil over high heat for 7 to 10 minutes, stirring often. Add the wine and cook until the liquid has evaporated, about 3 or 4 minutes. Add the chicken stock and cook over moderately high heat until the liquid is reduced by one half, about 10 minutes. Add the peppers, snow peas, and butter and cook over moderate heat until the peppers are tender, about 5 minutes. Taste and adjust for salt and pepper.

Hearts of Romaine Salad with Shaved Parmesan and Figs Page 121

SMOKED DUCK
AND GOOSE RAVIOLI

*Hearts of Romaine Salad with
Shaved Parmesan and Figs*
*Smoked Duck and Goose Ravioli
with Snow Pea and Red Pepper
Ragout*

Chardonnay or Chablis

This lively tasting dish uses smoked turkey, although any smoked fowl would be fine. Serve the beans on the side or use them on the tostada as the recipe suggests. Soft tortillas can be substituted for fried ones if you prefer soft tacos. *Crema* is a Latin cultured cream very similar to crème fraîche or sour cream. *Queso fresco* is a very young, crumbly white cheese, sometimes salty, but always very mild in flavor. Both foods can be found in Latin American markets. Substitute farmer's cheese or any other young cheese if you cannot find the true Mexican version.

Serves 6 to 8

Smoked Turkey Tostadas with Salsa Cruda

Vegetable oil
12 to 16 corn tortillas
Smoky Black Beans, following
2 cups shredded lettuce
2 cups shredded smoked turkey breast
1½ cups crumbled *queso fresco* (Mexican fresh white cheese) or
    farmer's cheese
2 cups Salsa Cruda, page 40
1 cup *crema*, crème fraîche, page 120, or sour cream

In a large sauté pan or skillet, heat a thin layer (⅛ inch) of oil over moderately high heat until hot but not smoking. Add 1 tortilla and cook until crisp around the edges; turn and cook on the other side until the edges are crisp and the tortilla is still slightly soft in the center. Remove to drain on paper towels and keep warm; repeat for remaining tortillas. Place the tortillas on individual plates. Top with some of the hot beans, then a bit of lettuce, turkey, cheese, and Salsa Cruda. Garnish with a drizzle of *crema*. Serve at room temperature.

Smoky Black Beans

If you would like to serve the beans on the tostadas drain them well; then you may mash them slightly with a fork if desired. If the beans are to be served as a side dish, the moisture need not be drained completely.

1½ cups dried black beans
7 cups water
½ pound bacon
1 large onion, cut into small dice
3 garlic cloves, minced
2 teaspoons *each* ground cumin and ground coriander
1 large tomato, peeled and chopped
Salt and pepper to taste

Sort, wash, and soak the beans in water to cover overnight, changing the water 2 times.

Drain the beans and place them with the 7 cups of water in a large pot; bring to a boil. Immediately reduce the heat to moderate and cook for 1½ to 2 hours or until the beans are very tender.

Meanwhile, cook the bacon in a large skillet until crisp. Remove the bacon from the skillet with a slotted spoon and drain on paper towels. Discard (or save for another use) all but ¼ cup of the fat. When the bacon is cool enough to handle, chop coarsely and set aside.

Add the onion, garlic, cumin, and coriander to the bacon fat in the pan and cook over moderate heat for 15 minutes, stirring from time to time. Add the tomato and cook 15 minutes.

When the beans are done, drain off any excess liquid and combine with the onion mixture and the reserved bacon; mix well and adjust the seasoning for salt and pepper.

Minted Orange and Jícama Salad

This is a refreshing salad, especially in warmer weather. It is also low in calories and fat.

1 small red onion, very thinly sliced
1 medium jícama, peeled and cut into julienne
Orange Vinaigrette, page 45
2 bunches watercress, stemmed
2 oranges, peeled and sectioned
¼ cup chopped fresh mint
Black pepper to taste

Combine the onion and jícama in a medium bowl. Dress with the vinaigrette and let stand at room temperature for at least 1 hour or up to 3 hours. Drain before serving.

Arrange the watercress on individual plates or a large platter. Top with the onion-jícama mixture and garnish with the orange sections and chopped mint. Sprinkle with pepper and serve at room temperature.

SMOKED TURKEY TOSTADAS
WITH SALSA CRUDA

Smoked Turkey Tostadas with
Salsa Cruda
Smoky Black Beans
Minted Orange and Jícama Salad

Oregon Pinot Noir

Wild turkey is leaner and more muscular than the domesticated variety; therefore it requires less cooking and the addition of fat, which in this case is thick slices of bacon. This menu allows for leftovers for turkey sandwiches and soup. Double the recipes for accompanying dishes if you plan to use the whole turkey for one meal.

Serves 6

Roast Wild Turkey with Cranberry-Apricot Glaze

Each slice of turkey takes on a subtle flavor of bacon, orange, and onion, but it is the Cranberry-Apricot Glaze that really adds a unique, sweet-tart taste to the crispy skin and meat.

1 medium onion, halved
1 orange, halved
One 10- to 12-pound wild turkey
Ground black pepper to taste
½ pound thickly sliced bacon
Cranberry-Apricot Glaze, page 43

Preheat the oven to 500°. Place the onion and orange in the cavity of the turkey and dust the outside with black pepper. Cover the turkey breast and legs with the bacon, truss the turkey, and place on a V-shaped rack in a greased roasting pan.

Cook for 15 minutes and immediately reduce the heat to 375°. Cover with aluminum foil and baste occasionally with the pan drippings. Cook 15 to 20 minutes to the pound, or until a turkey leg feels very loose when wiggled. Brush with the glaze during the last 1 hour of cooking.

Remove the turkey from the oven and let stand for 20 minutes before carving. Brush one last time with the glaze before serving.

Braised Turnips and Carrots

A splash of vanilla adds an unusual flavor to this classic vegetable combination.

3 shallots, minced
3 tablespoons unsalted butter
4 turnips, peeled and quartered if small, or cut into eighths if large
3 carrots, peeled and sliced into ½-inch-thick rounds
1½ cups rich homemade chicken or duck stock or canned low-salt chicken broth
1 teaspoon vanilla extract
¼ cup minced fresh parsley
Salt and pepper to taste

In a medium saucepan, cook the shallots in the butter over low heat for 5 minutes, stirring occasionally. Add the vegetables and cook over high heat for 1 minute. Add the chicken stock, reduce the heat to moderately low, and cook until the vegetables are tender, about 20 minutes. Add the vanilla extract and parsley; mix well. Taste and season with salt and pepper.

Sautéed Crispy Garlic Spinach

A large sauté pan or skillet and hot oil are all you need to make delicious sautéed spinach. Duck fat or even bacon fat would be a good substitute for the olive oil.

4 tablespoons olive oil
6 garlic cloves, peeled and thinly sliced
2 large bunches fresh spinach, washed, stemmed, and thoroughly dried
Juice of 1 lemon
Salt and pepper to taste

In a large sauté pan, skillet, or wok, warm the olive oil over high heat. Add the garlic and cook until golden brown. Add the spinach and cook over high heat for 10 seconds, stirring all the while, or until the spinach just begins to wilt. Add the lemon juice, salt, and pepper and serve immediately.

ROAST WILD TURKEY WITH CRANBERRY-APRICOT GLAZE

Roast Wild Turkey with Cranberry-
Apricot Glaze
Braised Turnips and Carrots
Sautéed Crispy Garlic Spinach

Zinfandel

POMEGRANATE-MARINATED GRILLED CHICKEN BREASTS

*Pomegranate-marinated Grilled
Chicken Breasts*

Cracked Wheat with Walnuts

*Sautéed Artichoke Hearts, Red
Pepper, and Fennel*

Beaujolais-Villages

This menu draws its inspiration from the Middle East. Be sure to purchase big, plump breasts from free-range chickens and have the butcher remove the bones when you buy them or do it yourself at home. Preboned breasts are often dry and have less flavor, so the longer you keep the meat attached to the bone, the better the finished dish will taste.

Serves 4

Pomegranate-marinated Grilled Chicken Breasts

2 large whole free-range chicken breasts, boned
Pomegranate Marinade, page 38
Pomegranate seeds for garnish

Place the chicken in a shallow non-aluminum pan, pour the marinade over, and turn chicken to coat evenly. Cover and marinate overnight. Wild-pheasant breasts may be substituted for the chicken breasts.

Prepare a fire in an open grill. When the coals are medium-hot, place the chicken, skin side down, on the grill and cook 7 to 8 minutes. Turn and cook the second side until tender, about 7 minutes, depending on the thickness of the fillets. Remove from the grill and let stand for 5 minutes before serving. Garnish with a few pomegranate seeds.

Cracked Wheat with Walnuts

Simple and easy to prepare, this Middle Eastern grain has a slightly sweet, nutty flavor. Choose medium-grained wheat for the most interesting texture.

1 medium onion, cut into small dice
2 tablespoons chicken fat or olive oil
1 cup cracked wheat
2 cups homemade chicken stock or canned low-fat chicken broth
½ cup walnuts, toasted and chopped
Salt and pepper to taste

In a large sauté pan or skillet, cook the onion in the fat over high heat for 10 minutes. Add the wheat and cook over high heat for 3 minutes, stirring all the while. Add the chicken stock and bring to a boil. Reduce the heat to low and cook until all the liquid is absorbed and the wheat is fluffy and slightly chewy, about 20 to 25 minutes. Add the walnuts and fluff with a fork. Season with salt and pepper.

Sautéed Artichoke Hearts, Red Pepper, and Fennel

Kalamata olives give this winning mint-scented vegetable combination a pleasantly salty taste. Use a fruity extra-virgin olive oil for this dish.

3 medium artichokes
¼ cup fresh lemon juice or white wine vinegar (optional)
3 tablespoons olive oil
1 small red bell pepper, cored, seeded, and cut into julienne
1 small fennel bulb, trimmed and cut into ½-inch-thick slices
2 garlic cloves, thinly sliced
¼ cup Kalamata olives, pitted and chopped
3 tablespoons chopped fresh mint
Salt and pepper to taste

Trim the stem and cut ½ inch off the top of each artichoke. Peel away the leaves until you get to the tender yellow inner leaves. Quarter the artichokes and remove the fuzzy choke. If the quartered artichokes are a bit large, cut each quarter in half. If you are not going to cook the artichokes right away, store them in water to cover mixed with the lemon juice. Drain before cooking.

Cook the artichokes in boiling salted water to cover until tender, about 7 minutes, depending on the size. Drain on paper towels and set aside.

Heat the oil in a large sauté pan or skillet over high heat. Add the pepper and fennel and cook over high heat, stirring constantly, for 2 minutes. Add the garlic, artichokes, and olives and cook over moderately high heat for 2 minutes, stirring constantly. Remove from the heat and stir in the mint. Season with salt and pepper.

ROAST LEMON-ROSEMARY CHICKEN

Roast Lemon-Rosemary Chicken
Sautéed Cucumbers with Feta
Cheese and Mint
Garlic-roasted New Potatoes

Sauvignon Blanc

Serve this menu for a fall picnic or casual supper. Rosemary, lemon, mint, Kalamata olives, and feta cheese give these dishes a Greek flavor. If you don't have enough time to marinate the chicken, simply drizzle it with fresh lemon juice and place a few sprigs of rosemary and a whole lemon in the cavity of the chicken before roasting. An adult pheasant may be substituted for the chicken.

Serves 4

Roast Lemon-Rosemary Chicken

One 5- to 6-pound free-range chicken
Lemon-Rosemary Marinade, page 38

Truss the chicken and place it in a shallow, non-aluminum pan, pour the marinade over, and turn chicken to coat evenly. Cover and marinate overnight in the refrigerator. Remove the chicken from the marinade and drain slightly.

Preheat the oven to 450°. Place the chicken on a V-shaped rack in a greased roasting pan and cook for 15 minutes. Reduce the heat to 375° and roast until the juices run clear when the underside of the chicken is pierced with a fork, about 1 to 1½ hours. Remove the chicken from the oven and let stand for 10 minutes before carving.

Sautéed Cucumbers with Feta Cheese and Mint

This refreshing vegetable dish can also be served uncooked. Simply combine all the ingredients in a bowl and mix well.

1 small red onion, very thinly sliced
3 tablespoons olive oil
1 large cucumber, halved, seeded, and cut into ½-inch-thick slices
⅓ pound feta cheese, crumbled
3 tablespoons coarsely chopped fresh mint
Salt and pepper to taste

Cook the onion in the oil over high heat for 3 minutes, stirring constantly. Add the cucumber, reduce the heat to moderate, and cook until the cucumber is just tender, about 3 to 4 minutes. Add the cheese and mint and stir just to mix. Taste and adjust for salt and pepper.

Garlic-roasted New Potatoes

Squeeze the soft, sweet garlic out of its casing and spread on the potatoes or chicken.

¼ cup olive oil
12 to 16 small new potatoes, halved
2 large *heads* garlic, cloves separated but not peeled
Salt and pepper to taste

Preheat the oven to 400°. Heat the oil in a heavy sauté pan or skillet. When the oil is hot, add the potatoes and brown on the cut sides. Transfer the potatoes and oil to a shallow baking pan and add the garlic. Place in the oven and cook until the potatoes and garlic are tender, about 45 minutes to 1 hour. Season with salt and pepper.

GRILLED CORNISH GAME HENS WITH TWO-MUSTARD SAUCE

Grilled Cornish Game Hens with
Two-Mustard Sauce
Wild Rice-Mushroom Pancakes
Sautéed Parsley Carrots

German Riesling

Tender young game hens are perfect for grilling. Their delicate meat and crispy skin make this an irresistible meal. These birds can dry out quickly, so be sure to watch them closely as they grill.

Serves 6 to 8

Grilled Cornish Game Hens with Two-Mustard Sauce

You may use poussins or even small fryer chickens in place of the game hens. The poussin has a larger breast than the game hen, but both have delicate and tender meat. Squab or baby pheasant may also be substituted.

6 Cornish game hens, split
Red Wine Marinade, page 39
Two-Mustard Sauce, page 40

Place the hens in a shallow non-aluminum pan, pour the marinade over, and turn the hens to coat evenly. Cover and marinate overnight in the refrigerator or for 2 hours at room temperature, turning occasionally.

Prepare a fire in an open grill. When the coals are medium-hot, place the birds, skin side down, on the grill. Cook, turning once, until the skin is golden brown and the juices run clear when the underside is pierced with a fork, about 7 to 9 minutes per side. Remove from the grill and let rest for 5 minutes before serving. Serve with Two-Mustard Sauce.

Wild Rice-Mushroom Pancakes

Serve any leftover pancakes at room temperature for brunch or lunch with a green salad and some sweet-hot mustard.

¾ cup raw wild rice, or 2 cups cooked wild rice
2 quarts water (optional)
1 large onion, finely diced
3 garlic cloves, minced
½ teaspoon *each* dried oregano, sage, basil, and thyme
4 tablespoons unsalted butter
½ pound white cultivated mushrooms, coarsely chopped
10 shiitake mushrooms, thinly sliced
2 tablespoons olive oil
3 tablespoons soy sauce
¼ cup minced fresh parsley
5 eggs, separated
½ to ¾ cup all-purpose flour
¼ pound *each* Italian fontina cheese and Parmesan cheese, grated
Olive oil for cooking pancakes

Wash the raw wild rice and cook it in the 2 quarts of boiling water until the grains are tender and beginning to burst, about 45 minutes to 1 hour. The rice should be slightly chewy but tender. Drain and set aside in a large bowl.

In a sauté pan or skillet, cook the onion, garlic, and herbs in the butter over moderately low heat until the onions are translucent, about 20 minutes. Add to the rice.

In the same pan, cook the mushrooms in the olive oil over high heat until golden brown, stirring often, about 5 to 7 minutes. Add to the rice and onion mixture. Add the soy sauce and parsley and mix well.

In a medium bowl, beat the egg yolks until smooth. In a large bowl, beat the egg whites until they form stiff peaks but are not dry. Set aside.

Add ½ cup of the flour, the egg yolks, and both cheeses to the mushroom-rice mixture; mix gently. Gently fold in the egg whites, mixing just until incorporated. (The whites make the fritters light, so do not overmix.)

Pour a thin film of oil into a large, nonstick sauté pan or skillet and place over moderate heat. When the oil is hot, carefully spoon the batter into the pan, using about 2 rounded tablespoons for each pancake. Do not crowd the pan. Cook over moderate heat until golden brown on the first side. Flip the pancakes and cook on the second side until golden brown. If the first pancakes seem to need more binding or if they are very fragile and difficult to flip, you may need to add the remaining flour to the batter, mixing gently. Remove the cooked pancakes with a slotted spatula and drain on paper towels. Keep warm in a low oven until all the pancakes are cooked. Serve hot.

Sautéed Parsley Carrots

This complex menu calls for a simple vegetable dish. Sautéed carrots tossed with fresh parsley add color and texture to the accompanying dishes.

3 large carrots, peeled, halved lengthwise and cut into ½-inch-thick
   diagonal slices
1 tablespoon unsalted butter
¼ cup minced fresh parsley
Salt and pepper to taste

Blanch the carrots in boiling salted water for 2 minutes. Drain and dry on paper towels.

Melt the butter in a large sauté pan or skillet over moderate heat, add the carrots and cook over high heat, stirring constantly, for 1 minute. Add the parsley, season with salt and pepper, and serve immediately.

Capons are known for their tender, slightly chewy meat and excellent flavor. Long cooking in liquid makes this large bird particularly tender, and the infusion of herbs helps to make a robust and satisfying dish.

Serves 6 to 8

Capon Stew with Winter Vegetables and White Beans

Hearty winter root vegetables contribute body and rich flavor to this aromatic stew. You may take the meat off the bones as the finished stew cools, or serve it on the bone in large, shallow soup bowls. Spoon the beans on top of the stew as garnish or mix them into the stew at the last minute. Either way, the beans must be cooked separately so that they retain their shape and have a distinctive flavor.

An adult pheasant or 2 to 3 grouse may be used in place of the capon.

1 capon, 6 to 7 pounds, cut into serving pieces
3 tablespoons chicken fat or olive oil
1 cup dry white wine
1 teaspoon *each* dried oregano, basil, thyme, and sage
3 cups chopped peeled tomatoes
4 cups homemade chicken stock or canned low-salt chicken broth
10 pearl onions, blanched for 30 seconds and peeled
2 turnips, peeled and cut into eighths
1 carrot, peeled and cut into ½-inch-thick diagonal slices
2 rutabagas, peeled and cut into eighths
Salt and pepper to taste
White Beans, following

Pat the capon pieces dry with paper towels. Melt the chicken fat in a large, deep kettle over moderate heat. Add the capon and fry, turning until golden brown on both sides. Add the white wine and cook over high heat until the wine evaporates, about 4 to 5 minutes. Add the herbs, tomatoes, and 3 cups of the stock. Bring to a boil, reduce the heat to moderate, and cook for 1½ hours.

When the capon is tender, add the onions and cook until they are half done, about 10 to 15 minutes. Add the remaining vegetables and cook over moderate heat until all the vegetables are tender, about 20 to 25 minutes. You may remove the meat from the bones at this point and return the chunks of meat to the stew. Season with salt and pepper. Mix the White Beans into the stew, or serve the stew with the beans spooned on top as a garnish.

White Beans
2 cups dried white beans
5 cups water
4 cups homemade chicken stock or canned low-salt chicken broth
½ pound bacon, coarsely chopped
1 large onion, finely diced
4 garlic cloves, minced
1 teaspoon dried red pepper flakes
Salt and pepper to taste

Sort the beans, discarding any discolored ones. Combine the beans and the 5 cups water and soak overnight, changing the water 2 or 3 times.

In a large, heavy saucepan, combine the chicken stock and beans; bring to a boil. Reduce the heat to moderately low and simmer until tender, but not mushy, about 1 to 1½ hours.

Meanwhile, cook the bacon in a sauté pan or skillet until crispy and golden brown. Remove the bacon with a slotted spoon and drain on paper towels. Reserve the bacon fat in the skillet. When the bacon is cool, crumble and set aside until ready to use.

Cook the onion, garlic, and red pepper flakes in the bacon fat over moderate heat until the onion is soft, about 15 minutes. Add the onion and bacon to the cooked beans and mix well. Taste and adjust for salt and pepper.

Fennel-Beet Salad with Orange Vinaigrette
Page 122

CAPON STEW WITH WINTER VEGETABLES AND WHITE BEANS

Capon Stew with Winter
Vegetables and White Beans
Fennel-Beet Salad with Orange
Vinaigrette

Chardonnay

This fast, easy pasta dish can be made with any leftover fowl, but the tender, flavorful meat of the poussin makes an outstanding dish. Squab or Guinea fowl can be substituted for poussin. Serve the savory tomatoes as an appetizer or along with the pasta.

Serves 4

Roast Poussin with Walnut–Goat Cheese Pasta

Top-quality olive oil forms the base of the pasta sauce. The other ingredients absorb the oil, lightening its overall effect.

4 poussins
Bacon fat or olive oil for rubbing on birds
2 onions, thinly sliced
6 garlic cloves, thinly sliced
⅔ cup olive oil
½ cup Madeira wine
1 yellow bell pepper, cored, seeded, and cut into julienne
¾ pound fresh linguine, or ½ pound dried linguine
1 bunch spinach, stemmed and cut into ¼-inch ribbons
¾ pound goat cheese, crumbled
1 cup walnuts, toasted and chopped
Salt and pepper to taste

Preheat the oven to 400°. Rub the birds with bacon fat and place them on a flat rack in a greased roasting pan. Roast until golden brown, about 25 to 30 minutes; remove from the oven and let cool. When cool enough to handle, remove the meat, with the crispy skin attached, from the bones and cut into small chunks. Set aside.

In a very large sauté pan or skillet, cook the onions and garlic in the olive oil over high heat for 10 minutes, stirring frequently. Add the Madeira, reduce the heat to moderate, and cook until the liquid evaporates, about 10 minutes. Add the bell pepper and cook until tender, about 2 minutes. Add the chopped poussin, remove from the heat, and set aside.

Cook the pasta in boiling salted water until al dente, about 2 minutes for fresh pasta or 8 to 10 minutes for dried. Drain well. Place in a very large mixing bowl with the spinach. Reheat the poussin mixture and add to the pasta along with the goat cheese and toss. (The spinach will wilt and the cheese will melt slightly from the heat of the pasta mixture.) Add the walnuts, toss, and season with salt and pepper. Serve immediately.

Duxelles-filled Tomatoes

The skins of these tomatoes may break slightly during the baking process. If you find this unattractive, peel the tomatoes before stuffing them. To slip the skins off easily, drop the tomatoes into boiling water for 5 to 15 seconds, depending on how ripe they are, remove them from the boiling water, and immediately plunge them into cold water. The skins will come right off. Mushroom soy sauce can be found in Asian markets and some natural foods stores. It is dark and syrupy and has a concentrated mushroom flavor.

4 large tomatoes
1 large onion, finely diced
2 garlic cloves, minced
1½ teaspoons *each* chopped fresh oregano, basil, thyme, and sage, or
  ½ teaspoon *each* dried
½ cup olive oil
½ cup dry sherry
2 pounds mushrooms, minced
½ cup seasoned finely ground bread crumbs
3 tablespoons mushroom soy sauce or soy sauce
Salt and pepper to taste

Preheat the oven to 350°. Cut a ½-inch slice off the top of each tomato. Carefully scoop out the pulp and seeds of the tomatoes, leaving only the shell. Discard the pulp and turn the tomatoes upside down to drain on paper towels.

In a large sauté pan or skillet, cook the onion, garlic, and herbs in the olive oil over moderate heat, stirring from time to time, for 15 minutes. Add the sherry and cook over high heat until the liquid evaporates, about 3 minutes. Remove from the pan with a slotted spoon and place in a bowl.

Cook the mushrooms in the remaining oil left in the pan. Cook over high heat until the mushrooms are golden brown. Add the bread crumbs and mushroom soy sauce and mix well. Add the mushrooms to the onions and mix. Taste and season with salt and pepper.

Spoon the filling into each tomato and place in a lightly greased roasting pan. Bake until the tomatoes are tender and filling is hot, about 15 to 20 minutes. Serve immediately.

Mixed Greens with Balsamic Vinaigrette
Page 122

GRILLED GIN-MARINATED
GUINEA FOWL

Grilled Gin-marinated Guinea
Fowl
Creamy Parsnip and Potato Gratin
Sautéed Mixed Vegetables with
Juniper Berries

Bandol or Rioja

A Guinea fowl has a large, juicy breast similar in taste to that of chicken. The legs and thighs have moist, slightly chewy dark meat with lots of flavor reminiscent of duck or goose. Gin marinade adds a bit of sweetness, which complements the juniper berries in the vegetables.

Serves 6

Grilled Gin-marinated Guinea Fowl

3 guinea fowl, about 2 pounds each, butterflied
Gin Marinade, page 38

Place the birds in a non-aluminum pan, pour the marinade over, and turn to coat the birds evenly. Cover and marinate overnight in the refrigerator. Remove the birds from the marinade and drain slightly.

Prepare a fire in an open grill. When the coals are medium-hot, place the birds on the grill, skin side down, and cook for about 10 minutes. Turn and cook on the second side for about 10 minutes, or until the skin is golden brown and the juices run clear when the underside is pierced with a fork. Remove from the grill and let rest for 5 minutes before serving.

Creamy Parsnip and Potato Gratin

This decadently creamy potato and parsnip dish is excellent the next day. You may use rutabagas or turnips instead of parsnips if you like.

3 red boiling potatoes, peeled and cut into ¼-inch-thick slices
2 parsnips, peeled and cut into ¼-inch-thick slices

1 medium onion, very thinly sliced
2 to 3 cups heavy cream
3 garlic cloves, minced
1 tablespoon ground coriander
1½ teaspoons salt
1 teaspoon ground black pepper
1 pound semi-firm cheese, such as Bel Paese, Havarti, or Fontina, shredded

Arrange the potatoes, parsnips, and onion in layers in a 12-inch sauté pan or skillet.

Combine the cream, garlic, coriander, salt, and pepper; mix well. Pour the cream mixture over the vegetables. Cook over moderately low heat until the potatoes and parsnips are very tender, about 45 minutes to 1 hour. Sprinkle the cheese over the top and heat until the cheese is melted, about 5 to 7 minutes. Serve immediately.

Sautéed Mixed Vegetables with Juniper Berries

½ pound green beans, trimmed
2 carrots, peeled and thinly sliced
2 yellow crookneck squash, halved and cut into ½-inch-thick slices
1 tablespoon chicken fat or olive oil
1 tablespoon olive oil
1 teaspoon juniper berries, crushed
Salt and pepper to taste

In separate saucepans, cook the green beans and carrots in boiling salted water until almost tender, 4 to 5 minutes for the beans and about 2 minutes for the carrots. Remove from the water and drain on paper towels. In a sauté pan or skillet, cook the squash in the chicken fat and olive oil over high heat for 2 minutes. Add the green beans, carrots, and juniper berries. Cook over high heat for 1 or 2 minutes, stirring often. Season with salt and pepper and serve immediately.

This festive grill menu draws inspiration from the piquant flavors of Mexico. Ancho peppers, dusky and deep flavored, add a unique taste to the finished squab. If your grill is not big enough to accommodate all the vegetables and the squab, cook the squab first and let it rest while you cook the vegetables. Like all cooked meat, it will benefit from a short period of resting.

Serves 4 to 6

Grilled Lime-and-Ancho-marinated Squab

The marinade adds a unique flavor to these tasty birds.

6 to 8 squabs, split
Lime and Ancho Pepper Marinade, page 38

Place the squabs in a large, shallow non-aluminum pan and pour the marinade over them, turning to coat evenly. Refrigerate for 8 hours or overnight, turning several times. Remove from the marinade and drain slightly before cooking.

Prepare a fire in an open grill. When the coals are medium-hot, place the squabs on the grill, skin side down. Cook, turning once, until tender and golden brown, 7 to 10 minutes on each side, depending on the heat of the grill. Remove from the grill and cover with aluminum foil.

Chorizo Gorditas

These golden brown discs filled with spicy Mexican sausage are delicious all on their own, but they truly complement the squab and grilled vegetables in this menu. Masa harina is a flour made from ground corn and sold in Latin American markets, natural foods stores, and some grocery stores.

Makes 30 to 35 gorditas

5 russet potatoes, peeled and cut into eighths
1 tablespoon ground coriander
1 teaspoon ground black pepper
½ teaspoon salt
⅓ pound sharp Cheddar cheese, grated
½ cup masa harina
1 teaspoon baking powder
⅓ pound chorizo or firm spicy sausage
Olive oil for frying gorditas

Cook the potatoes in salted boiling water to cover for 35 to 40 minutes, or until tender. Drain, cool, place in a large bowl, and mash with a potato masher or with your hands. Add the coriander, pepper, salt, and cheese and mix well. Add the masa harina and baking powder and mix to form a soft but pliable dough. Cover and refrigerate for 3 or 4 hours or overnight.

Cut the chorizo into slices about ½ inch thick. Place a piece of chorizo in the center of your palm. Take about 2½ tablespoons of dough and form it around the sausage, enclosing it on all sides. Slightly flatten the dough to form a small patty. Repeat with the remaining sausage and dough. Cover and refrigerate for at least 1 hour.

Over moderately low heat, warm a thin film of oil in a large nonstick skillet. Working in batches, add the patties and cook, turning once, until golden brown on both sides, about 5 minutes per side. Remove from the pan and serve immediately, or keep warm in a low oven until ready to serve.

Grilled Tomatoes, Onions, Mushrooms, and Zucchini with Allspice-Mace Butter

Easy and quick to prepare, this side dish gets a final glaze of spice butter. The butter should be at room temperature so that it melts on the vegetables.

12 cherry tomatoes
12 medium mushrooms
2 medium sweet onions, sliced ½ inch thick
1 large zucchini, sliced ½ inch thick on the diagonal
Olive oil for brushing
Allspice-Mace Butter, page 43, at room temperature

Thread the tomatoes and mushrooms on separate skewers, leaving about ⅛ inch between each piece. Brush all the vegetables with a little olive oil. Place the onion slices on the grill first and cook over medium-hot coals until they begin to turn golden brown, about 5 minutes per side. Place the zucchini and mushrooms on the grill and cook about 5 minutes per side or until tender and juicy. Add the tomatoes and cook about 2 minutes. Remove all the vegetables from the grill and immediately slip the vegetables off the skewers. Brush the hot vegetables with the Allspice-Mace Butter and serve immediately.

Tequila-Steamed Clams
Page 120

GRILLED LIME-AND-ANCHO-MARINATED SQUAB

Tequila-steamed Clams
Grilled Lime-and-Ancho-
marinated Squab
Chorizo Gorditas
Grilled Tomatoes, Onions,
Mushrooms, and Zucchini with
Allspice-Mace Butter

Côtes du Rhône

Serve this colorful fall meal for company or a family gathering. The tiny, delicate birds are crispy on the exterior and tender inside because they cook in just a few minutes. Plan on 2 quail per person for moderate or big eaters and just 1 for small eaters.

Serves 6

Tomato-Red Pepper Bisque

Although this bright red soup needs little in the way of garnish, a swirl of crème fraîche or a sprig of cilantro or parsley would make a stunning addition. The soup takes about an hour to prepare, but tastes even better reheated the next day.

1 large red onion, thinly sliced
3 garlic cloves, chopped
3 large red bell peppers, chopped
1 tablespoon ground coriander
1 teaspoon dried oregano
½ cup (1 stick) unsalted butter
¼ cup dry sherry
3 large tomatoes or 2 cups chopped tomatoes
5 cups homemade chicken stock or canned low-salt chicken broth
½ cup half and half
Salt and pepper to taste
Minced fresh parsley or cilantro, for garnish

In a large soup pot, cook the onion, garlic, peppers, and herbs in the butter over moderately high heat for 10 minutes. Add the sherry, tomatoes, and chicken stock and bring to a boil over high heat. Reduce the heat and cook over moderate heat for 30 minutes. Remove from the heat and cool.

Puree the tomato mixture in a blender or food processor until smooth. Strain through a fine sieve and return to the pot. Add the cream and bring to a boil. Reduce the heat to moderately low and cook for 15 to 20 minutes. The soup should have the consistency of heavy cream. If the soup is too thin, cook it over high heat, stirring frequently, until it thickens. Season with salt and pepper and garnish with parsley or cilantro.

Grilled Quail with Honey-Hazelnut Sauce

Delicate in texture but big in flavor, quail is perfect for grilling. If you cook the birds for 5 minutes, the breasts will still be slightly pink and the legs will be cooked all the way through.

12 quail
Red Wine Marinade, page 39
Honey-Hazelnut Sauce, page 39

Place the birds in a shallow non-aluminum pan, pour the marinade over, and turn to coat evenly. Cover and marinate in the refrigerator overnight or for up to 2 days turning several times. If pressed for time you can marinate for only 2 hours at room temperature.

Prepare a fire in an open grill. When the coals are medium-hot, place the quail on the grill and cook until golden brown, about 5 to 7 minutes per side. Remove from the grill and drizzle with the sauce. Serve immediately.

Sweet Potato Croquettes

These golden brown sweet potato nuggets can also be served for breakfast, drizzled with maple syrup.

1 large onion, finely diced
3 tablespoons unsalted butter
1 green apple, finely diced
½ teaspoon ground nutmeg
1 teaspoon ground coriander
2½ cups cooked mashed sweet potato (about 4 large sweet potatoes)
1 egg, lightly beaten
Juice from 1 lemon
Salt and pepper to taste
All-purpose flour for coating
2 eggs, lightly beaten
2 cups fine dried bread crumbs
Olive oil for cooking

Cook the onion in the butter over moderate heat for 10 minutes, stirring occasionally. Add the apple, nutmeg, and coriander and cook 2 more minutes.

Combine the onion mixture with the sweet potato, 1 beaten egg, lemon juice, salt, and pepper in a bowl; mix well. Cover and refrigerate for at least 1 hour or up to 2 days.

Form the sweet potato mixture into small cylindrical shapes, using about 3 tablespoons for each croquette. Coat each piece with flour. Dip in the eggs, taking care to coat the croquette completely. Roll in the bread crumbs to coat thoroughly. Refrigerate for at least 1 hour or cover and refrigerate for up to 1 day.

Heat about ½ inch oil in a shallow nonstick skillet over moderate heat. When the oil is hot but not smoking, add the croquettes in batches and cook, turning frequently, until golden brown on all sides, about 3 to 4 minutes. Remove with a slotted spoon or spatula and keep warm in a low oven until all the croquettes are cooked. Serve hot.

Sautéed Green and Wax Beans
Page 120

GRILLED QUAIL WITH HONEY-HAZELNUT SAUCE

Tomato-Red Pepper Bisque
Grilled Quail with Honey-
Hazelnut Sauce
Sweet Potato Croquettes
Sautéed Green and Wax Beans

Oregon or California Pinot Noir

ROAST SQUAB WITH BALSAMIC-PORT GLAZE

Roast Squab with Balsamic-Port
Glaze
Onion-Potato Cakes
Wilted Dandelion Greens with
Bacon and Garlic

Cabernet Sauvignon or
Haut-Medoc

These small flavorful birds are all dark meat, a treat for those who prefer a more intense flavor. As with other lean fowl, squab can dry out quickly, so take care not to overcook. The combination of the sweet-sour glaze on the squab with the bitter greens, sweet and crispy garlic and salty bacon strikes a perfect balance of flavors in this menu.

Serves 4 to 6

Roast Squab with Balsamic-Port Glaze

I prefer squab roasted to the point where it is still pink at the bone; the texture of the meat benefits from slight undercooking.

4 to 6 squabs
¼ cup bacon fat or olive oil
Ground black pepper to taste
Balsamic-Port Glaze, page 43

Preheat the oven to 450°. Truss the squabs and rub with bacon fat, then sprinkle with pepper. Place on a flat rack in a greased roasting pan and bake for 5 minutes. Reduce the heat to 400° and brush with the glaze. Roast, brushing with the glaze every 10 minutes, until the skin is golden brown and the juices run clear when a joint is pierced with a fork, about 20 to 25 minutes. Let rest for 5 minutes before serving.

Onion-Potato Cakes

The versatile potato is the perfect food for simple or complex flavoring. Here slightly caramelized onions and fresh chives combine for a two-dimensional taste.

3 large baking potatoes, peeled and cubed
2 onions, finely diced
2 garlic cloves, minced
3 tablespoons chicken fat or olive oil
¼ cup minced fresh chives
Salt and pepper to taste
2 eggs, lightly beaten
1½ cups fine dried bread crumbs
Olive oil for cooking

Cook the potatoes in boiling salted water to cover until very tender, about 40 minutes. Drain and place in a bowl to cool. Mash the potatoes with a fork.

In a large sauté pan or skillet, cook the onions and garlic in the chicken fat over high heat for 10 minutes, stirring often. Reduce the heat to moderate and cook for 10 minutes, stirring occasionally, or until the onions are golden brown. Remove from the heat and add to the potatoes. Add the chives, salt, and pepper; mix well. Refrigerate the mixture for at least 1 hour or up to 2 days.

Form the potato mixture into pancakes about 2 inches in diameter and ½ inch thick. Dip in the egg wash and dust with bread crumbs.

Heat about ¼ inch olive oil in a large nonstick sauté pan or skillet. When the oil is hot but not smoking, add the potato cakes, being careful not to crowd the pan. Cook over moderate heat until golden brown on one side, about 3 or 4 minutes. Flip the cakes, using a spatula, and cook the second side until golden brown. Remove with a slotted spatula and drain on paper towels. Keep the potato cakes warm in a low oven until all are cooked. Serve hot.

Wilted Dandelion Greens with Bacon and Garlic

Dandelion greens can be quite bitter, especially when they are mature, so search out tender, young leaves. Add spinach if you are not fond of such an intense flavor. Or substitute spinach or escarole for half of the dandelion greens.

¼ pound sliced bacon
8 garlic cloves, thinly sliced
1 large bunch dandelion greens, chopped into 3-inch lengths
Juice of 1 lemon
½ cup pine nuts, toasted
Salt and pepper to taste

In a large sauté pan or skillet, cook the bacon until it is crisp. Remove from the pan with a slotted spoon and drain on paper towels. Pour off all but 3 tablespoons bacon fat. When the bacon is cool, chop coarsely and set aside.

Cook the garlic in the bacon fat over moderate heat until it is golden brown and slightly crispy, about 3 minutes. Remove with a slotted spoon and set aside.

Heat the fat remaining in the pan. Over high heat cook the dandelion greens for about 1 minute, stirring all the while. Add the lemon juice, browned garlic, cooked bacon, pine nuts, salt, and pepper. Mix well and serve immediately.

SQUAB WITH PISTACHIO NUT-SAUSAGE STUFFING

Squab with Pistachio Nut-Sausage
Stuffing
Basmati Rice
Baked Acorn Squash with Lemon

Barolo or Barbaresco

Squab is the perfect little "holder" for a rich, savory stuffing. The boned birds aren't very large, but the wonderful dark meat is delicious. You may use any small bird with the bone in, but this boneless preparation is a bit more elegant and simpler to eat.

Serves 8

Squab with Pistachio Nut-Sausage Stuffing

Normally 2 squabs per person is a good idea, but this stuffing is so rich and filling that 1 bird per person is enough in this menu.

8 whole squabs, boned
Pistachio Nut-Sausage Stuffing, page 46
Madeira Sauce, page 40

Preheat the oven to 400°. Fill the squabs with the stuffing just before cooking. Tie the legs together and wrap the flap of skin around the underside of the squabs. Place on a flat rack in a greased roasting pan.

Roast for 30 minutes. Reduce the heat to 350° and cook until the juices run clear when the underside of a squab is pierced with a fork, about 10 to 15 minutes. Serve each bird with a drizzle of Madeira Sauce.

Basmati Rice

This aromatic rice is commonly found in Indian and Southeast Asian kitchens. You may find it in a natural foods, gourmet, ethnic, or large grocery store. If not, substitute any long-grain white rice.

3 cups basmati or long-grain white rice
4 quarts water
¼ pound unsalted butter
¾ cup minced fresh parsley and/or cilantro
Salt and pepper to taste

Rinse the rice until the water runs clear. Bring the 4 quarts of water to a boil in a large pot. Add the rice and return the water to a boil. Reduce the heat to moderate and cook until the rice is just tender, but not mushy, about 15 minutes. Drain in a sieve and place in a large shallow bowl. Add the butter in small chunks, along with the parsley, salt, and pepper. Toss with a fork and serve immediately.

Baked Acorn Squash with Lemon

This golden squash is a favorite at Thanksgiving time, but why reserve it only for special holidays? It is usually partnered with butter, but this recipe calls only for a bit of olive oil for cooking and a drizzle of fresh lemon juice just before serving.

4 acorn squashes, quartered and seeded
Olive oil for rubbing on squash
Juice of 2 lemons
Salt and pepper to taste

Preheat the oven to 400°. Cut each quarter squash into half-moon shapes approximately ½ to ¾ inch thick. Rub with olive oil and place on a greased baking sheet. Bake in the oven for 15 to 20 minutes, or until the squash is tender but not mushy. Remove from the oven, drizzle with lemon juice, and season with salt and pepper.

This simple meal is wonderful to make for company, as it requires little last-minute attention. The partridge is a slightly chewy bird that benefits from long, slow cooking. Herb-infused lentils make a moist and flavorful bed for the bird, and the assorted vegetables add color and texture to the plate.

Serves 6

Braised Rosemary Partridge with Lentils

French green lentils are best for this dish because they hold their shape particularly well when cooked; however, they are sometimes difficult to find. Red lentils may be substituted.

¼ cup chicken or duck fat
4 partridges (1 pound each), split
½ cup dry sherry
1 teaspoon minced fresh rosemary
1 tablespoon minced fresh oregano
3 tomatoes, peeled and chopped
5½ cups homemade chicken stock or canned low-salt chicken broth

Lentils
1 onion, finely diced
4 garlic cloves, minced
1 teaspoon *each* dried thyme and basil
2 tablespoons bacon or chicken fat or olive oil
1 cup green or red lentils, sorted and rinsed
3 cups homemade chicken stock or canned low-salt chicken broth
Salt and pepper to taste
Flat-leaf parsley or rosemary sprigs for garnish

In a large saucepan, melt the fat over moderate heat. Add the partridges and cook over high heat until golden brown on all sides, about 3 to 5 minutes. Add the sherry and herbs and cook over high heat until the sherry evaporates, about 2 to 3 minutes. Add the tomatoes and chicken stock and bring to a boil over high heat. Reduce the heat to moderate and cook, uncovered, for 30 minutes. Cover and cook until the meat is tender when pierced with a fork, about 1 hour. While the birds are cooking, prepare the lentils.

To cook the lentils: In a large saucepan, cook the onion, garlic, and herbs in the fat over moderately low heat for 10 minutes. Add the lentils and chicken stock and bring

to a boil. Reduce the heat to moderate and cook until lentils are tender but not mushy, about 15 to 20 minutes. Season with salt and pepper.

To serve, spoon some lentils onto individual plates or a large platter. Place the partridges on top of the lentils and garnish with parsley or rosemary.

Sauté of Artichokes, Leeks, and Carrots

This is one of my favorite vegetable dishes. The combination of flavors complements the creamy lentils and lean partridge. Try to find baby or very small artichokes; they are easier to work with and are more attractive in this dish than the larger variety.

6 medium or 12 baby artichokes
¼ cup fresh lemon juice or distilled white vinegar
3 medium carrots, peeled and cut into ¼-inch diagonal slices
2 small leeks, halved and cut into ½-inch slices
¼ cup olive oil
¼ cup dry white wine
Salt and pepper to taste
Pinch dried red pepper flakes

Trim the stems and cut 1½ inches from the top of the medium artichokes or 1 inch from the baby artichokes. Peel away the leaves until you get to the tender inner yellow leaves. Discard the outer leaves. Halve the baby artichokes or quarter the medium ones. Remove any fuzzy choke from the large artichokes. Add the lemon juice or vinegar to enough boiling salted water to cover the artichokes and cook the artichokes over moderately high heat until tender but not mushy, about 5 minutes. Drain on paper towels.

Cook the carrots in boiling salted water to cover until tender, about 5 minutes. Drain and dry on paper towels.

Cook the leeks in the olive oil over moderate heat for 5 minutes. Add the wine, carrots, and artichokes and cook over high heat until the liquid evaporates, about 2 minutes. Season with salt, pepper, and red pepper flakes and serve immediately.

BRAISED ROSEMARY PARTRIDGE WITH LENTILS

*Braised Rosemary Partridge with Lentils
Sauté of Artichokes, Leeks, and Carrots
Rioja or Chianti Classico*

ROAST SNOW GROUSE

Roast Snow Grouse
Herbed Rice Pilaf
Sautéed Asparagus and Snow
Peas
Savigny-les-Beaunes

If you like poultry or game with a very pronounced flavor, or if you adore dark meat, then this small bird is for you. Although not large, snow grouse have quite a bit of meat, especially breast meat. Their dark red flesh is quite lean, so cooking with added fat is a must. If properly cooked the meat remains moist, flavorful, and tender.

Serves 6

Roast Snow Grouse

Bacon adds flavor and moisture to these lean birds. Be sure the bacon completely covers the breasts as the grouse cook.

6 to 10 snow grouse, depending on size
Ground black pepper to taste
12 slices bacon

Preheat oven to 400°. Truss the grouse and sprinkle them with black pepper. Place a strip of bacon over the breast of each bird. Place the birds on a flat roasting rack in a greased roasting pan and roast until tender, about 25 to 30 minutes. Remove from the oven and let rest for 5 minutes before serving.

Herbed Rice Pilaf

A classic rice dish, this delicate pilaf is full of rich chicken flavor and fresh herbs. Serve any leftovers at room temperature the next day with a few cooked vegetables added for color and texture.

1 medium onion, finely diced
2 garlic cloves, minced
3 tablespoons butter or duck fat
1 tablespoon olive oil
1½ cups long-grain white rice
3½ cups homemade chicken stock or canned salt-free chicken broth
⅓ cup minced mixed fresh herbs such as parsley, chives, oregano, and thyme
Salt and pepper to taste

In a medium, heavy saucepan, cook the onion and garlic in the butter and oil over high heat for 10 minutes. Add the rice and cook for 3 to 4 minutes, stirring constantly. Add the chicken stock and bring to a boil. Reduce the heat and cook, covered, until the rice is tender and the liquid has been absorbed, about 20 to 25 minutes. Add the herbs and fluff with a fork. Season with salt and pepper.

Sautéed Asparagus and Snow Peas

This summery vegetable duo is bright and lively and takes only minutes to prepare. Be sure to remove any strings from the snow peas.

2 pounds asparagus, trimmed and cut into 1½-inch diagonal slices
1 tablespoon unsalted butter
¾ pound snow peas, trimmed

Blanch the asparagus in boiling salted water for 30 seconds. Drain and dry well on paper towels. Melt the butter in a sauté pan or skillet. When the butter is melted, add the asparagus and snow peas and cook over high heat until the peas are bright green and both vegetables are tender but still crisp, about 1 minute. Serve immediately.

BRAISED RABBIT WITH FENNEL, OLIVES, AND ORANGES

Mixed Greens with Goat Cheese
and Dates
Braised Rabbit with Fennel,
Olives, and Oranges
Fried Polenta Triangles

Graves or Sauvignon Blanc

This "blond" stew is light and subtle. Different types of rabbit require different cooking times, but generally speaking, a stewing rabbit, usually twice the size of a fryer, needs long, slow cooking with plenty of liquid.

Serves 4 to 6

Braised Rabbit with Fennel, Olives, and Oranges

This stew is even better the second day. You may use a combination of pitted Kalamata and green olives if you wish.

½ pound sliced bacon
1 stewing rabbit, 4 to 5 pounds, cut into serving pieces
Olive oil if needed for browning
2 bay leaves
1 teaspoon *each* dried basil, oregano, sage, and thyme
6 to 8 cups rich homemade chicken stock or canned low-salt chicken broth
1 large onion, sliced
6 garlic cloves, thinly sliced
3 tablespoons olive oil
Juice of 2 oranges
1 large fennel head, trimmed and sliced
1 cup Greek or Italian green olives
Zest of 1 orange
¼ cup minced fresh parsley
Salt and pepper to taste

Cook the bacon in a heavy sauté pan or skillet until almost crisp. Remove with a slotted spoon and drain on paper towels. Reserve the fat. When the bacon is cool, chop coarsely.

In the same pan, cook the rabbit in batches in the bacon fat, adding olive oil if necessary. Brown the rabbit on all sides and set aside. Place all the browned pieces of rabbit in a large kettle. Add the bay leaves, herbs, and 3 cups of the stock and bring to a boil. Reduce the heat to moderate and cook for 1½ hours. Add 3 more cups of stock and continue cooking over moderate heat until the meat is very tender and starts to fall off the bones. Let cool and remove the meat from the bones. Return the meat to the cooking liquid in the kettle, if any remains. If not, add 2 cups of stock.

In a medium saucepan, meanwhile cook the onion and garlic in the olive oil over moderately high heat for 10 minutes, stirring occasionally. Add the orange juice and cook over moderate heat for 5 more minutes. Add the onion mixture, fennel, and olives to the rabbit with the remaining stock. Bring to a boil, reduce the heat to moderate, and cook until the liquid has almost evaporated and the meat is very tender. Add the bacon, zest, parsley, salt, and pepper.

Fried Polenta Triangles

These triangles of polenta with cheese form a golden brown crust when they are grilled in a little olive oil. Allow plenty of time for the polenta to set in the refrigerator before it is fried.

5 cups water
3 garlic cloves, minced
5 tablespoons unsalted butter
2 teaspoons salt
1 teaspoon ground white pepper
1¾ cups polenta
¾ pound Italian Fontina or Bel Paese cheese, shredded
Olive oil for cooking

Bring the water, garlic, butter, salt, and pepper to a boil in a large, heavy saucepan. Slowly add the polenta, whisking all the while. Bring the mixture to a boil and immediately reduce the heat to moderately low, whisking all the while. Cook the polenta, stirring with a wooden spoon every 3 or 4 minutes, for 15 to 20 minutes, or until the grains are small and soft and the color is pale yellow. When the polenta is done, add the cheese and stir to incorporate. Pour the hot polenta into a 9-by-12-inch baking pan and smooth to make an even surface. Refrigerate for at least 8 hours or overnight, covered with plastic wrap.

With a small knife, cut the polenta into medium triangles. Remove these from baking pan carefully so as not to break them.

Heat a thin film of olive oil in a large nonstick sauté pan or skillet. When the oil is hot but not smoking, add the pieces of polenta and cook over moderate heat until golden brown on both sides, about 5 to 7 minutes per side. Cook in batches, keeping the cooked polenta warm in a low oven. Serve hot.

Mixed Greens with Goat Cheese and Dates
Page 122

Rabbit is a very delicate meat that reminds some people of chicken. The ratio of meat to carcass is less than that of chicken, however, so plan accordingly when purchasing. The meat is very lean and can be dry if cooked too long with dry heat. Marinating the meat adds flavor and moisture, but attention to cooking times is particularly important for this dish.

Serves 4 to 6

Grilled Rabbit with Prune-Cognac Sauce

1 rabbit, 4 to 4½ pounds, cut into serving pieces
Red Wine Marinade, page 39
Prune-Cognac Sauce, page 42

Place the rabbit in a shallow non-aluminum pan, pour the marinade over, and turn to coat the pieces evenly. Marinate the rabbit overnight or for up to 2 days, turning several times. Remove from the marinade and drain slightly before cooking.

Prepare a fire in an open grill. When the coals are medium-hot, place the rabbit, skin side down, on the grill and cook until the juices run clear, about 10 to 12 minutes per side, depending on how hot the coals are. Remove from the grill and allow to sit for 5 minutes before serving. Serve with a drizzle of Prune-Cognac Sauce.

Golden Disc Potatoes

These potatoes might cook through just by being browned. If this is the case, simply keep them warm in a low oven until all of them have been browned.

Olive oil for cooking
5 large baking potatoes, cut into ½-inch-thick slices
Salt and pepper to taste

Preheat the oven to 350°. Heat about ¼ inch of oil in a large nonstick sauté pan or skillet. Add the potatoes in batches and cook over moderate heat until golden brown on both sides, adding more oil if necessary. Remove with a slotted spatula and place on a sheet pan. Bake until tender all the way through. Season with salt and pepper.

Sautéed Chard with Carrots

The deep rose stems of red chard make a stunning addition to the green leaves and golden carrot slivers.

1 large bunch chard
2 carrots, peeled
2 tablespoons chicken fat or olive oil
6 garlic cloves, thinly sliced
Juice of 1 lemon
Salt and pepper to taste

Cut off the stems of the chard; slice the stems on the diagonal into 1-inch lengths. Cut the chard into 3-inch-wide pieces. Cut the carrots into slivers: Slice the carrots into diagonal slices about 1 to 1½ inches long and ⅛ inch thick. Stack 3 slices of carrot on top of each other and, using a very sharp knife, cut into ⅛-inch-thick pieces. Blanch the carrots and chard stems in boiling salted water to cook for 1 minute. Drain and dry thoroughly on paper towels.

Melt the chicken fat in a large sauté pan or skillet over high heat. Cook the garlic for 1 minute, stirring constantly. Add the chard and cook for 1 minute, stirring all the while. When the chard just starts to wilt, add the stems and carrots and cook for about 30 seconds. Add the lemon juice, salt, and pepper and serve immediately.

GRILLED RABBIT WITH PRUNE-COGNAC SAUCE

Grilled Rabbit with Prune-Cognac
Sauce
Golden Disc Potatoes
Sautéed Chard with Carrots

Zinfandel or Dolcetto

Venison is one of the more popular varieties of game and rightly so, as it is intense but not too gamey in flavor. Any type of venison, including deer, moose, elk, or reindeer, may be used for this stew, and beef or pork may be substituted if venison is unavailable. This menu draws inspiration from American and Mexican cuisines and makes a substantial fall meal.

Serves 6

Corn Cakes with Red Pepper-Ancho Sauce

Light and delicate, these corn cakes are the perfect appetizer. The deep red, slightly spicy sauce contrasts nicely with the yellow cakes.

1 cup unbleached all-purpose flour
1 teaspoon salt
1 tablespoon ground coriander
2 large eggs, separated
3 tablespoons butter, melted
1 cup milk
¼ cup minced fresh chives
2 cups corn kernels (about 2 or 3 large ears of corn)
Olive oil for cooking
Red Pepper-Ancho Sauce, page 42
Flat-leaf parsley sprigs for garnish

Combine the flour, salt, and coriander in a large bowl. Combine the egg yolks, melted butter, and milk. Add slowly to the dry ingredients, stirring constantly to make a smooth batter. Add the chives and mix. Refrigerate for at least 1 hour or overnight.

Add the corn to the batter and mix well. Beat the egg whites until they form stiff peaks. Fold into the batter.

Heat a thin layer of olive oil in a large nonstick sauté pan or skillet. When the oil is hot but not smoking, add the batter, using about 2 tablespoons for each cake. Cook over moderate heat until golden brown on both sides. Serve hot with the Red Pepper-Ancho Sauce and garnish with sprigs of parsley.

Venison Stew with Wild Rice and Dried Apricots

As is the case with most stews, this one is even better the second day. Make the rice just before serving. The nutty taste of wild rice is a sensational match with dried apricots.

½ pound sliced bacon
2½ pounds venison, cut into 1-inch cubes
All-purpose flour for dredging
1 cup dry red wine
1 tablespoon ground fennel seed
4 cups homemade beef stock or canned low-salt beef broth
2 onions, cut into medium slices
5 garlic cloves, cut into thin slices
Salt and pepper to taste
2 quarts water
1½ cups wild rice, washed
4 tablespoons unsalted butter
1 cup dried apricots, cut into thin slices
Minced fresh parsley for garnish

In a large sauté pan or skillet, cook the bacon until almost crisp. Remove with a slotted spoon and drain on paper towels. When cool, chop coarsely. Remove half of the bacon fat to a large pot.

Dredge the meat in the flour. Heat the bacon fat in the large pot and cook the meat over high heat until brown on all sides. Add the wine and cook over high heat, scraping the bottom of the pan, until the wine has evaporated, about 3 to 4 minutes. Add the fennel seed and beef stock and bring to a boil over high heat. Reduce the heat to low and cook until the meat is very tender, about 2½ to 3 hours.

Meanwhile, cook the onions in the remaining bacon fat in the first pan over high heat for 10 minutes, stirring occasionally. Add the garlic, reduce the heat, and cook over low heat for 30 minutes. When the meat is tender, add the cooked onions and garlic and the bacon. Season to taste.

In a stockpot, bring the 2 quarts water to a boil, add the wild rice, and cook for 40 to 45 minutes, or until the grains "burst." Drain thoroughly in a colander. Melt the butter in a large saucepan. Add the apricots and cook for 2 minutes. Add the rice and toss, using a fork. Season with salt and pepper.

Serve the stew on a bed of the rice and garnish with minced parsley.

Mixed Greens with Sherry Vinaigrette

6 cups mixed greens such as assorted lettuces, arugula, watercress, dandelion, escarole, mustard, and frisée
Sherry Vinaigrette, page 45

Wash and thoroughly dry the greens. Place in a large mixing bowl and drizzle with some of the vinaigrette. Toss and serve immediately.

**VENISON STEW WITH WILD RICE
AND DRIED APRICOTS**

Corn Cakes with Red Pepper-
Ancho Sauce
Venison Stew with Wild Rice and
Dried Apricots
Mixed Greens with Sherry
Vinaigrette

Cabernet Sauvignon or Barolo

BRAISED LEG OF WILD BOAR WITH BLACK BEANS AND CHILIES

Braised Leg of Wild Boar
with Black Beans and Chilies
Toasted Pumpkin Seed Rice

Fixin or Zinfandel

Leg of boar can be dry and tough if prepared improperly, but slow cooking in plenty of liquid assures a wonderful result. The presentation of chunks of meat with strips of peppers and tiny black beans is irresistible. Make this filling winter stew the day before you plan to serve it so that the flavors will deepen. Sweet potatoes or corn tortillas would be delicious with the meal.

Serves 6 to 8

Braised Leg of Wild Boar with Black Beans and Chilies

If you cannot find wild boar, use a leg of pork. Red or pinto beans can be substituted for the black beans. Whatever the final choice of ingredients, this nutritious stew will be satisfying and filling.

Beans
1½ cups dried black beans
1 large onion, finely diced
6 garlic cloves, minced
2 to 3 jalapeño chilies, cored, seeded, and minced
2 tablespoons bacon fat
6 cups water
2 bay leaves

3 tablespoons bacon fat
One 7- to 8-pound leg of boar
3 tablespoons ground coriander
1½ tablespoons ground cumin
1 tablespoon *each* dried oregano, sage, and marjoram
6 garlic cloves, thinly sliced
1 cup dry red wine
1 large carrot, peeled and thinly sliced
6 cups homemade beef stock or canned low-salt beef broth
3 cups chopped peeled tomatoes or one 28-ounce can peeled tomatoes
3 green Anaheim chilies, cored, seeded, and cut into ½-inch strips
2 red bell peppers, cored, seeded, and sliced into ½-inch strips
Salt and pepper to taste
1 small yellow bell pepper, cored, seeded, and cut into julienne for garnish (optional)

Sort the beans, discarding any discolored ones. Rinse and soak the beans in water to cover overnight, changing the water 2 times. In a large pot, cook the onion, garlic, and jalapeños in the bacon fat over moderate heat for 10 minutes, stirring occasionally. Add the beans, the 6 cups water, and bay leaves and bring to a boil. Reduce the heat to moderately low and cook, uncovered, until the beans are almost tender, about 30 to 45 minutes. Drain and set aside until ready to use.

Heat the remaining bacon fat in a heavy pot large enough to hold the boar leg. When the fat is hot, add the meat and cook over moderate heat until browned on all sides. Add the herbs, garlic, and red wine and cook until the liquid is gone. Add the carrot and beef stock and bring to a boil. Reduce the heat, cover, and cook over moderate heat for about 3 hours, stirring from time to time.

When the meat is tender, remove from the pot and allow to cool slightly. While the meat is cooling, reduce the liquid to about 4 to 5 cups. Remove the meat from the bones and return to the pot. Add the tomatoes, chilies, peppers, and cooked beans and bring to a boil. Reduce the heat to moderate and cook for 25 to 30 minutes or until the meat and beans are very tender. Season with salt and pepper, garnish with the yellow peppers if you like, and serve with the rice.

Toasted Pumpkin Seed Rice

This delicious Mexican-style rice is dotted with crunchy toasted pumpkin seeds. Cook the rice just before serving so it will be steaming hot. It makes a great bed for the hearty boar stew.

1 large onion, finely diced
2 garlic cloves, minced
3 tablespoons olive oil
2½ cups long-grain white rice
5¼ cups homemade chicken stock or canned low-salt chicken broth
Salt and pepper to taste
¾ cup chopped fresh cilantro
1 cup pumpkin seeds, toasted

In a large saucepan, cook the onion and garlic in the oil over moderate heat for 10 minutes, stirring frequently. Rinse the rice until the water runs clear. Add the rice to the onion and garlic and cook for 5 minutes, stirring frequently. Add the chicken stock and bring to a boil, stirring only once. Reduce the heat to moderate and cook, uncovered, for 15 minutes or until most of the liquid has been absorbed. Cover with a lid and cook 10 to 15 more minutes.

Remove from the heat and let the rice stand for 15 minutes. Add salt, pepper, cilantro, and toasted pumpkin seeds and toss with a fork. Serve immediately.

GRILLED BUFFALO STEAKS

Grilled Buffalo Steaks
Grilled Zucchini and Onions with
Cilantro-Jalapeño Butter
Fried Potatoes

Cabernet Sauvignon or Red
Bordeaux

This straightforward meal takes only minutes to prepare. Cumin, coriander, fresh cilantro, and fiery jalapeño chilies add a Southwest touch. Guacamole would be a good appetizer with this meal. Put the onions on the grill first as they take the longest.

Serves 6

Grilled Buffalo Steaks

Beef steaks may be substituted if you cannot find buffalo. The taste is similar, but the size and cut may differ.

6 New York strip buffalo steaks, 6 to 8 ounces each
Red Wine Marinade, page 39

Place the steaks in a non-aluminum pan and pour the marinade over, turning to coat each piece evenly. Marinate the steaks for at least 6 hours or overnight, turning several times. Drain slightly before cooking.

Light a fire in an open grill. When the coals are medium-hot, place the steaks on the grill and cook on one side for 2 to 3 minutes, turning the steaks at a right angle halfway through to make a cross-hatch pattern with the grill grids. Flip the steaks and cook on the second side till the desired doneness is achieved, preferably medium-rare (1 to 2 minutes).

The amount of time required to cook the steaks depends on the thickness and size of the meat and the intensity of heat from the coals. Remove from grill and let stand for 5 minutes before serving.

Grilled Zucchini and Onions with Cilantro-Jalapeño Butter

Grilled vegetables are simple and easy to prepare. Sweet and tender onions and bright green zucchini make a very satisfying side dish to any grilled meat.

8 medium onions, halved crosswise
8 medium zucchini, halved lengthwise
Olive oil for brushing on vegetables
Cilantro-Jalapeño Butter, page 43, softened
Salt and pepper to taste

Brush the cut side of the onions and zucchini with olive oil. Place the onions on the grill cut side down and cook, turning from time to time, until all sides are golden brown and the onions are tender, 15 to 20 minutes. Place the sliced zucchini cut side down on the grill and cook on both sides until tender, about 5 to 7 minutes.

Remove from the grill and place on a platter. Immediately brush with the softened Cilantro-Jalapeño butter, season, and serve.

Fried Potatoes

Old-fashioned fried potatoes are great, but spiked with ground spices they make a particularly wonderful companion to grilled steaks. If there are leftovers, serve them reheated for breakfast with scrambled eggs and chorizo.

12 medium red potatoes, cut into medium dice
¼ cup olive oil
1 tablespoon ground coriander
2 teaspoons ground cumin seed
2 teaspoons chili powder
Salt and pepper to taste

Cook the potatoes in boiling salted water to cover until they are half cooked, about 5 minutes. Drain and cool. (Do not run cold water over the potatoes; this makes them mushy.)

Heat the oil in a large sauté pan or skillet placed over moderate heat. When the oil is hot, add the potatoes and all the herbs and spices. Mix well and cook over moderate heat until the potatoes are golden brown on all sides and very tender, about 15 minutes. Serve immediately.

Note: To reheat for leftovers: Heat a thin film of olive oil in a large sauté pan or skillet. Add the potatoes and cook, stirring, over moderately low heat for about 5 minutes, or until warmed through. You may also heat them in a 350° oven until warmed, about 7 to 10 minutes.

ROAST VENISON STRIP LOIN
WITH WILD MUSHROOM SAUCE

Roast Venison Strip Loin with
Wild Mushroom Sauce
Garlicky Mashed Potatoes
Sautéed Fennel and Red Peppers

Barolo or Barbaresco

Venison loin is a dramatic and elegant dish for any dinner table. This cut of venison is very tender and flavorful, with absolutely no fat, gristle, or bone. Mashed potatoes and fennel round out a special fall meal.

Serves 6

Roast Venison Strip Loin with Wild Mushroom Sauce

A beef or pork tenderloin can be used if venison is difficult to find. The cooking times will vary, but I suggest cooking the meat medium-done for pork, and medium rare for beef and venison.

One venison strip loin (2½ to 3½ pounds)
3 tablespoons bacon fat or prepared mustard
3 garlic cloves, minced
2 teaspoons ground black pepper
Wild Mushroom Sauce, page 42

Preheat the oven to 450°. Pat the meat dry with paper towels. Combine the bacon fat, garlic, and black pepper in a small bowl; mix well. Rub the mixture on the meat and place it on a flat rack in a greased roasting pan. Roast for about 15 to 17 minutes for medium. Remove from the oven and allow to stand for 5 minutes before serving. Slice into ½-inch rounds and serve with the Wild Mushroom Sauce.

Garlicky Mashed Potatoes

Cooking the potatoes in milk adds extra flavor and moisture to the finished dish. Form any leftover potatoes into small patties and fry in a little olive oil until browned.

8 large baking potatoes, peeled and each cut into 6 pieces
1 quart water
1 quart milk
4 garlic cloves, minced
2 teaspoons salt
1 teaspoon ground black pepper
½ cup (1 stick) unsalted butter, cut into 8 pieces

Place the potatoes, water, milk, garlic, salt, and pepper in a large pot. Bring to a boil and stir well. Reduce the heat to moderate and simmer until the potatoes are very tender, about 30 to 35 minutes.

Drain most of the liquid from the potatoes, but leave enough so that the mixture looks wet and rather mushy. Gradually add the butter to the potatoes and mash with a hand masher until almost smooth. Taste and season with more salt and pepper if necessary. If the potatoes are too wet, heat them over a low flame, stirring occasionally, until they are stiffer. Watch carefully; they should not be too dry.

Sautéed Fennel and Red Peppers

Sweet fennel and red pepper is a pleasing combination that works well with wild mushrooms and roasted meats.

1 medium onion, cut into thin wedges
3 tablespoons olive oil
3 large fennel bulbs, sliced thin
1 large red bell pepper, cored, seeded, and cut into julienne
Salt and pepper to taste
¼ cup minced fresh parsley

Cook the onion in the olive oil over high heat for 3 minutes, stirring all the while. Add the fennel and pepper and cook 2 to 3 more minutes, or until the fennel is tender but not mushy. Season with salt and pepper, add the parsley, and serve immediately.

Extra Recipes

Tequila-steamed Clams

Choose any variety of fresh steamer clams for this light, healthy appetizer. Cherrystone, littlenecks, or Manila clams are all suitable for this dish. Generally speaking, seafood doesn't hold well, so be ready to serve the clams as soon as they open up.

4 to 5 dozen clams in the shell
⅓ cup salt
4 quarts water
1 medium onion, finely diced
5 garlic cloves, minced
1 jalapeño chili, cored, seeded, and minced
5 tablespoons unsalted butter
1 teaspoon ground black pepper
1½ cups homemade fish stock or bottled clam juice
¾ cup tequila

Scrub the clams under running cold water. Combine the salt and water, add the clams, and soak for 1 to 4 hours in the refrigerator. Drain and rinse with fresh water.

In a large pot, cook the onion, garlic, and jalapeño in the butter over moderate heat for 10 minutes, stirring frequently. Add the black pepper, fish stock, and tequila and bring to a boil. Cook for 1 minute over high heat.

Place the clams in the pot, cover tightly, and cook over moderate heat, shaking the pan from time to time, until all the clams are open, about 3 to 4 minutes. Discard any clams that do not open. Spoon the clams and juice into bowls and serve immediately.

Sautéed Green and Wax Beans

If you cannot find yellow wax beans use only green. Blue Lake beans are excellent, but any fresh green beans will do.

¾ pound green beans, trimmed
¾ pound yellow wax beans, trimmed
2 shallots, sliced thin
1 tablespoon unsalted butter
1 tablespoon olive oil
Salt and pepper to taste

Cook the beans in salted boiling water until almost tender, about 3 minutes. Drain and plunge them into ice water. Drain and dry on paper towels.

Cook the shallots in the butter and oil over low heat for 3 minutes. Add the beans and cook over high heat for 2 minutes. Season with salt and pepper.

Stir-fried Chinese Vegetables

The pan should be very hot and the oil smoking to cook these vegetables properly. A wok is ideal, but if you don't have one you can use a large, heavy skillet.

2 tablespoons vegetable oil
One 3-inch piece fresh ginger root, peeled and thinly sliced
5 garlic cloves, thinly sliced
2 cups broccoli florets
½ cup fresh or canned water chestnuts, thinly sliced
¼ cup homemade beef stock or canned low-salt beef broth
1 cup shredded Chinese cabbage
8 shiitake mushrooms, stemmed and halved
3 tablespoons soy sauce

Heat a large wok or heavy skillet and add the oil. When the oil is smoking, add the ginger, garlic, broccoli, and water chestnuts and cook, stirring constantly, for 2 minutes over high heat. Add the beef stock and cook over high heat for 1 minute. Add all the remaining ingredients and cook over high heat for 2 minutes. Serve immediately.

Winter Squash Soup with Orange Crème Fraîche

This soup is simple to make but the results are quite elegant. Canned squash can be used, but you might have to adjust the liquid, as it will be more watery than fresh squash.

1 large onion, chopped
2 garlic cloves, chopped
1 large carrot, finely chopped
1 tablespoon ground coriander
1 teaspoon ground mace
½ teaspoon ground cardamom
¼ pound unsalted butter
6 or 7 cups light homemade chicken stock or canned low-salt chicken broth
2 cups cooked winter squash (Hubbard, Danish, or acorn)
Salt and pepper to taste
½ cup Orange Crème Fraîche, page 40

Cook the onion, garlic, carrot, and spices in the butter over moderate heat for 20 minutes, stirring frequently. Add the chicken stock and squash and bring to a boil. Reduce the heat to moderate and cook 20 minutes, stirring frequently. When the mixture is cool, puree in a blender or food processor until smooth. You may add more chicken stock or water if necessary.

Return the soup to the pot and bring to a boil. Reduce the heat and season with salt and pepper. Serve with a swirl of Orange Crème Fraîche.

Sautéed Zucchini

Yellow summer squash may be used in place of zucchini, or you can cook some along with the zucchini for extra color.

3 tablespoons fruity olive oil
5 garlic cloves, thinly sliced
3 large zucchini, halved lengthwise and sliced ½ inch thick
1 tablespoon minced fresh oregano
Salt and pepper to taste

Heat the oil in a large sauté pan or skillet over moderate heat. When the oil is hot but not smoking, add the garlic and zucchini and cook for 3 to 4 minutes, stirring all the while. When the zucchini is tender but still bright green, add the oregano, salt, and pepper and serve immediately.

Carrot and Parsnip Soup with Orange

This silky, smooth soup is soothing and pleasantly sweet. Though it is delicious cold in the warm seasons, it should be served hot during the fall and winter months.

1 large onion, cut into medium dice
2 teaspoons ground coriander
1 teaspoon ground cumin seed
½ cup (1 stick) unsalted butter
1 cup dry white wine
4 carrots, cut into medium dice
3 parsnips, cut into medium dice
8 cups light homemade chicken stock or canned low-salt chicken broth
½ cup fresh orange juice
Pinch cayenne pepper
1 tablespoon sherry vinegar
Salt and pepper to taste
Minced fresh chives or parsley for garnish

Cook the onion, coriander, and cumin seed in the butter over moderate heat for 15 minutes. Add the white wine and cook until the wine evaporates, about 5 minutes. Add the carrots and parsnips and cook for 5 minutes. Add the chicken stock and bring to a boil. Reduce the heat to moderately low and simmer until the vegetables are tender, about 35 to 40 minutes. Remove from the heat and let cool slightly. Transfer the mixture to a blender or food processor and puree in batches until smooth. Return to the pot and add the orange juice, cayenne pepper, and vinegar and mix well. Bring to a boil, reduce the heat, and season with salt and pepper. Serve hot, garnished with chives or parsley.

Sautéed Green Beans

Prepare this timeless holiday vegetable dish with half yellow wax beans and half green beans, if you wish.

1½ pounds green beans, sliced ½ inch long on the diagonal
3 shallots, thinly sliced
2 tablespoons unsalted butter
Salt and pepper to taste

Cook the green beans in boiling salted water until they are al dente, about 3 minutes. Drain and plunge them into ice water. Drain and dry thoroughly on paper towels.
Cook the shallots in the butter over low heat for 5 minutes. Add the green beans and cook over high heat for 2 minutes. Season with salt and pepper and serve immediately.

Hearts of Romaine Salad with Shaved Parmesan and Figs

Parmegiano Reggiano is one of the finest cheeses available. Its almost sweet yet nutty taste, golden color, and dense texture are unsurpassed. If you cannot find this cheese, substitute Asiago or a very good Parmesan.

3 heads romaine lettuce
Balsamic Vinaigrette, page 45
8 dried figs, trimmed and thinly sliced
¼ pound Parmegiano Reggiano
Coarsely ground black pepper to taste

Remove all of the green outer leaves of the lettuce, leaving only the tender yellow inner leaves. Save the outer leaves for another occasion. Place the inner leaves in a large bowl and drizzle with the vinaigrette. Toss well and place on a platter or individual plates. Garnish with the figs. Using a vegetable peeler, shave thin slices of the cheese onto the top of the salad. Dust with coarsely ground black pepper and serve immediately.

Fennel-Beet Salad with Orange Vinaigrette

A colorful and lively salad, this makes a wonderful light lunch served with bread sticks or crackers. If you cannot find yellow beets use only red.

2 medium red beets
2 medium yellow beets
½ small red onion, sliced paper thin
½ cup rice vinegar
Zest of 1 orange
1 fennel bulb, thinly sliced
Orange Vinaigrette, page 45
1 large bunch watercress, stemmed
2 ounces Parmigiana Reggiano, shaved
Freshly cracked black pepper to taste

Cook the red and yellow beets separately in boiling water to cover until tender, about 35 to 40 minutes; drain and cool. Meanwhile, soak the onions in the rice vinegar for 20 minutes; drain.

Peel and quarter the beets or cut them into eighths. Combine the beets, orange zest, fennel, and onion in the vinaigrette and marinate for 1 to 3 hours at room temperature or in the refrigerator overnight.

Arrange the watercress on a large platter or individual plates. Spoon the marinated vegetables over the watercress. Using a vegetable peeler, shave thin pieces of the cheese over the vegetables. Dust with black pepper and serve at room temperature.

Mixed Greens with Balsamic Vinaigrette

Try to find baby lettuces such as green and red leaf, red oak, romaine, and butter, but if these tender little greens are not available use butter or leaf lettuce.

4 cups baby greens or other assorted lettuces
Balsamic Vinaigrette, page 45

If you are using baby greens, just separate the leaves; wash and dry. If you are using regular lettuce, tear the leaves into bite-sized pieces; wash and dry. Place the greens in a large bowl and drizzle with some of the vinaigrette. Toss gently and serve immediately.

Mixed Greens with Goat Cheese and Dates

Freezing pitted dates for at least an hour facilitates chopping or cutting.

6 cups mixed greens such as assorted lettuces, frisée, arugula, mustard,
    dandelion, endive, and watercress.
Balsamic Vinaigrette, page 45
⅓ pound goat cheese, crumbled
8 dates, pitted and coarsely chopped

Wash and thoroughly dry the greens. Place in a large bowl. Drizzle with some of the vinaigrette and toss. Place the greens on individual plates or a large platter. Garnish with the goat cheese and dates. Serve immediately.

SOURCES FOR GAME AND SPECIALTY FOODS

D'Artagnan
399–419 St. Paul Avenue, Jersey
City, NJ 07306
Telephone: 800-327-8246
Wild game and fowl, foie gras,
smoked game, duck fat.

Durham—Night Bird
650 San Mateo Avenue, San Bruno,
CA 94066
Telephone: 415-873-1940
Exotic produce, wild and domestic
mushrooms, gourmet food products,
wild game and fowl.

Foggy Ridge Gamebird Farm
P.O. Box 88, Thomaston, ME 04861
Telephone: 207-273-2357
Organic ring-necked pheasant,
chukar partridge, bobwhite quail.

The Game Exchange (retail);
Polarica Game USA (wholesale)
107 Quint Street, San Francisco,
CA 94188
Mailing Address: P.O. Box 880204
Telephone: 800 GAME USA or
415-647-1300
Wild game and fowl, foie gras,
exotic produce, wild and domestic
mushrooms, imported gourmet
products.

Wild Game
2315 West Huron Street, Chicago,
IL 60612
Telephone: 312-278-1661
Wild fowl, venison, buffalo, smoked
meat, poultry and fish, caviar, wild
mushrooms, gourmet food products.

BIBLIOGRAPHY

Audubon. *Birds of America*. New York: The Macmillan Company, 1950.

Beard, James. *James Beard Fowl and Game Bird Cookery*. New York: Harvest/ HBJ Books, 1979.

Becker, Marion Rombauer. *The Joy of Cooking*. New York: Bobbs-Merrill Company, 1975.

Gisslen, Wayne. *Professional Cooking*. New York: John Wiley and Sons, 1983.

Manion, Timothy. *Wild Game and Country Cooking*. Manion Outdoors Co., 1983.

Scott, Philippa. *Gourmet Game*. New York: Simon and Schuster, 1990.

Smith, John A. *Wild Game Cookbook*. New York: Dover Publications, 1986.

Stuart, Charles E. *Game Cookbook*. Virginia: The Country Publishers, 1982.

INDEX